# SEARCH PARTY

Books by William Matthews

# SEARCH PARTY

COLLECTED POEMS OF

# William Matthews

Edited by

## Sebastian Matthews

and

## Stanley Plumly

HOUGHTON MIFFLIN COMPANY

Boston   New York   2004

For information about permission to reproduce selections from
this book, write to Permissions, Houghton Mifflin Company,
215 Park Avenue South, New York, New York 10003.

Visit our Web site: www.houghtonmifflinbooks.com.

*Library of Congress Cataloging-in-Publication Data*

Matthews, William, 1942–1997
Search party : collected poems of William Matthews /
edited by Sebastian Matthews and Stanley Plumly.
    p. cm.
Includes index.
ISBN 0-618-35007-1
I. Matthews, Sebastian, 1965–   II. Plumly, Stanley.   III. Title.

PS3563.A855A17    2004
811'.54—dc22    2003056795

Book design by Anne Chalmers
Typefaces: Venetian 301 (Bitstream), Centaur, Humanist

Printed in the United States of America

MP 10 9 8 7 6 5 4 3 2

Some of these poems have not appeared before in book form. We would like to thank the
editors of the journals in which they first appeared: *Afterthought:* Gossip. *Amicus Journal:*
Names. *Atlantic Monthly:* E lucevan le stelle. *Ironwood:* Leaving the Cleveland Airport. *New England
Review:* Jilted. *Passages North:* Grandmother Talking. *Plainsong:* Clearwater Beach, Florida,
1950. *Poetry:* The Buddy Bolden Cylinder; Grandmother Dead at 99 Years and 10 Months;
Portrait of the Artist as a Young Clarinetist. *Quarterly West:* Driving Through the Poconos,
Route 80, 1:30 A.M., Snow. *Sand Hills Press:* A Walk with John Logan, 1973. *Seattle Review:*
Dancing to Reggae Music. *Solo:* Condoms Then; The Memo. *Tar River Review:* Phone Log.
*TriQuarterly:* Another Real Estate Deal on Oahu. *Virginia Quarterly Review:* Slow Work.

    "Gossip" and "Leaving the Cleveland Airport" originally appeared in *Provisions: The Lost
Prose of William Matthews*, a limited edition, hand-set book from Sutton Hoo Press.

for Peter Davison

# CONTENTS

## Sticks & Stones

## Rising and Falling

## Flood

## Uncollected Poems (1967–1981)

## A Happy Childhood

## Foreseeable Futures

## Blues If You Want

## Time & Money

## Uncollected Poems (1982–1997)

## After All

# INTRODUCTION

THE POEMS in this collection represent the best of William Matthews's ten original books of poetry, almost thirty years' worth, beginning in 1970 and including the posthumous *After All,* 1998. There are some hundred and sixty-five poems here, twenty-six of which are from work previously unpublished in a book. In the course of his remarkable career, Matthews placed in various magazines — from the ephemeral to *The Atlantic Monthly* and *The New Yorker* — more than eight hundred poems. He was prolific, but he was also selective. When it came time to assemble a new volume, he was severe. Either a poem played in concert with the concept of the whole manuscript or it didn't. Fewer than half the poems he wrote made it into books.

With the help of Michael Collier, Houghton Mifflin's poetry consultant, and Peter Davison, Matthews's longtime friend and editor, Sebastian Matthews and I have followed the author's model in producing a collection we feel he would be proud of, a selection he himself might have made. Matthews died on November 12, 1997, the day after his fifty-fifth birthday. He had, just days before, sent off the completed manuscript of *After All,* in accordance with a creative schedule that presented a new book of poetry every three years. Added to this calendar were any number of critical essays, commentaries, memoir pieces, reviews, and interviews, many of which have been gathered into *Curiosities* (1989) and *The Poetry Blues* (2001).

Matthews's marvelous letters make up yet another category. His correspondence with the world, through his masterly poems and graceful prose, was rich and varied; his correspondence with his friends and acquaintances was loving, engaging, and always on point. All of Matthews's writing, regardless of genre, reveals the man, both the persona he wished to disclose and the person he almost successfully kept to himself. His brilliance and volubility are inseparable from his reserve—the tension between them is the core dynamic of his kinetic mind and demanding language. His announced self and secret self parley not only the precision of his diction and imagination but the spoken music of his sentence. His poetry, like his prose, can seem impromptu, when in fact it is written in astute, rehearsed internal conversation within a form itself being addressed. Matthews's buoyant feel for analysis, his restless curiosity, his refreshing range of knowledge, his quirky, often sardonic take on memory, his insistence on the invisibility of his craft—these elements and more set him apart as a maker.

To paraphrase, however, is only to suggest Matthews's depth and resonance as a poet. The implicit chronology of this careful selection of his poems conjures a narrative of work that moves from the imagistic, aphoristic seventies to the more directly autobiographical eighties to the more meditative, introspective nineties. All the while the poems grow in size, texture, complexity, darkness, and acceptance of the given situation—or, at the least, a reluctant reconciliation. The full heart behind the poems becomes more and more available to the luminous mind making them. Too often honored for his wit alone, the Matthews throughout these pages is a poet of emotional resolve, enormous linguistic and poetic resources, and, most especially, a clarifying wisdom. Here he is reinforced as a writer of responsibility to form and tradition as well as irony and idiom, whether that heritage refers to literature, jazz, and epicurean delight or elegiac testimonies for those he has loved.

Reading Matthews you get the impression that his insights and images and the syntax created by his inevitable ear have traveled great distances to the page. They have. They arrive distilled from a metaphysics in which thought is not only feeling but a coherent language, a language that must be mastered before it can be made. "Snow Leopards at the Denver Zoo," from the seventies, is an early example.

## Snow Leopards at the Denver Zoo

There are only a hundred or so
snow leopards alive, and three
of them here. Hours I watch them jump

down and jump up, water being
poured. Though if you fill a glass
fast with water, it rings high to the top,
noise of a nail driven true. Snow
leopards land without sound,
as if they were already extinct.

If I could, I'd sift them
from hand to hand, like a fire,
like a debt I can count but can't pay.
I'm glad I can't. If I tried to
take loss for a wife, and I do,
and keep her all the days of my life,
I'd have nothing to leave my children.
I save them whatever I can keep
and I pour it from hand to hand.

    The connections in this poem easily surpass discrete metaphor to become the total medium—submersion—through which they move: from the snow leopards to water to snow to fire to consuming debt to loss; from jumping to pouring to filling to counting to pouring . . . the concentric circles derive from and return directly to their common center of gravity in a flow and speed almost preternatural. Then there is the touch of the "nail driven true," the exquisite understatement of the soundlessness of the leopards, landing "as if they were already extinct," and the reality of taking "loss for a wife." The fragility of the poem is also its subject, the balance of saving "whatever I can keep" against the perishability of losing it all. Behind the poem is the certain knowledge—which is a theme in Matthews's poetry—that it will all, always, slip through our hands. This genius for turning the most familiar materials into something extraordinary—both smart and moving at once—comes from his gift for making connections and exploiting them to the limit their language will bear.
    For all the normal changes in his writing, as Matthews matured he never surrendered his talent for the fragile, mortal moment that quickens the feel of things. At times his tone may have sharpened—he loved Byron as much as he loved Martial—but he never gave in to the fragmentary, the broken, the piecemeal hard emotion. He was

continually a writer of the controlled but complete embrace. I think the soul of his work is closer to the toughness and sweetness of Horace, to the passions of mind of Coleridge, and to the nocturnal blues melancholy of all those jazzmen he revered. He grew up in Ohio, within the margins of both country and small city, pastoral and postwar urban. His father worked for the Soil Conservation Service. He rode a bike, had a newspaper route (the *Dayton Daily News*), went to the county fair, played baseball and basketball, moved back to Cincinnati (his birthplace), then later to a larger, eastern, Ivy League world. A not uncommon midwestern American story. Yet he never lost his sense of humor about himself nor forgot where he came from. His complexity combined the Ohioan and the New Yorker, the boy and the man, beautifully in his poetry.

In the transitional sixties, when he was a graduate student in Chapel Hill, Matthews met Russell Banks, also in graduate school and also starting out as a writer. They soon collaborated on what became one of the exceptional small literary magazines of its era, *Lillabulero*. The collaboration would fade but the friendship would last a lifetime. Matthews's commitment to the small magazine would not fade. It says everything about him that a good portion of the poems in this collection first appeared in journals of often very short shelf lives. He became one of the premier poets of his generation, yet he remained faithful to the idea of where literature can find its first expression. His democratic instincts never failed him. Matthews was preeminently fair-minded, and this egalitarian spirit informed every part of his personality and permitted him to serve vital roles in American poetry culture at a vital time, from the Poetry Society of America to the National Endowment for the Arts. And his tireless support of younger writers, it goes without saying, began with his superb teaching.

It is still difficult, for many of his friends and admirers, to believe that he is gone. The poems represented here are alive in ways and at depths that most poetry can at best aspire to. The intimacy is never too familiar, the conversation never too friendly, the imagination never too busy, the wit never too sterling. The fault lines of heartbreak are everywhere, yet they map an intact emotion. Every gesture, every turn, every reverse is guided and governed by a classicism that values moderation, generosity, and, at just the right moment, an utter truth. Timing, indeed, is essential to Matthews's internal music: he knows just when to smile, when to open the window, when to change the pace, and when the last line is the last line. And he knows he knows, without display. Reading this collection, front to back or intermittently at leisure, we love his mind, we celebrate the skill that lifts the quotidian to meaning. And we love, even more, the man whose life was so much at stake in the words.

STANLEY PLUMLY

# Ruining the New Road

## (1970)

# The Search Party

I wondered if the others felt
as heroic
and as safe: *my* unmangled family
slept while I slid uncertain feet ahead
behind my flashlight's beam.
Stones, thick roots as twisted as
a ruined body,
what did I fear?
I hoped my batteries
had eight more lives
than the lost child.
I feared I'd find something.

Reader, by now you must be sure
you know just where we are,
deep in symbolic woods.
Irony, self-accusation,
someone else's suffering.
The search is that of art.

You're wrong, though it's
an intelligent mistake.
There was a real lost child.
I don't want to swaddle it
in metaphor.
I'm just a journalist
who can't believe in objectivity.
I'm in these poems
because I'm in my life.
But I digress.

A man four volunteers
to the left of me
made the discovery.
We circled in like waves
returning to the parent shock.
You've read this far, you might as well
have been there too. Your eyes accuse
me of false chase. Come off it,
you're the one who thought it wouldn't
matter what we found.
Though we came with lights
and tongues thick in our heads,
the issue was a human life.
The child was still
alive. Admit you're glad.

# Psychoanalysis

Everything is
luxurious; there is no past,
only an oceanic present.
You troll along in your glass-
bottomed boat.
Parents and siblings lurk
among the coral with thick eyes,
they will not eat you
if you understand them
well enough. Stop,
you whisper to the ingratiating
pilot, here we are,
maybe this means an end
to all those hours listlessly improvising.
Letting down
the line you think maybe
now you have it,
it will come up slick
with significance, laden
with the sweet guilt you can name.

# Blues for John Coltrane, Dead at 41

Although my house floats on a lawn
as plush as a starlet's body
and my sons sleep easily,
I think of death's salmon breath
leaping back up the saxophone
with its wet kiss.

Hearing him dead,
I feel it in my feet
as if the house were rocked
by waves from a soundless speedboat
planing by, full throttle.

# Coleman Hawkins (d. 1969), RIP

As if that sax
were made of bone wrenched from his wrist
he urged through it dank music
of his breath. When he blew ballads
you knew one use of force:
withholding it.
This was a river of muscles.
Old dimes oily from handling,
eggs scrambled just right in a diner
after eight gigs in nine nights,
a *New Yorker* profile, a new Leica
for the fun of having one.
Gasps and twitches.
It's like having the breath
knocked out of me
and wearing the lost air for a leash.
I snuffle home.
I hate it that he's dead.

# Jealousy

1
Now I have this smoking coal
I'm growing from carbon
in my gut,
a snake hoping to sleep off
his meal of fire.
My heart enters a half-life
of sludged pumping.

2
This lump, this pearl I am making
sometimes jumps
                        like a burning bee.
Black honey!

3
This way love dies
                        somewhere else,
like an arm wriggled out of its sling.

4
If I rasp like a crashing plane,
like a ground-down spine
made into a rhythm instrument,
it is because I am knitting
a fern of bone for your thigh,
Oh
        I wish it were so,
I'd take my stubbled tongue
and file these words
                        down
to their nub of curse.

5
In the dewy grass, first July light,
I blurt damp balls of breath up,
suck them back in.
                    Well hell
I shall be warm
by my own fire
though the sun come.

# Moving

When we spurt off
in the invalid Volvo
flying its pennant of blue fumes,
the neighbors group and watch.
We twist away like a released balloon.

# Lust

It is a squad car idling
through my eyes, bored,
looking for a crime to crush.
Two tough cops drive it,
three years on the same beat,
sick of each other.
To it I am no better
than a radish.
I hear its indolent engine
grump along in second gear,
feel both cops watch me
walk with stiff ankles,
a nun among drunks.

# Faith of Our Fathers

Now it is time to see what's left:
not much.
Gulls above the scrub pine, the tufted dunes —
though nothing visible emits that low, slurred moan —,
the graves in rows like a tray full of type.
What we have lost
you may guess by what we have kept.
We rise to sing
like beach grass swaying in the wind.
O hymn of salt, the pages of the hymnal
riffling, turning
at last by themselves.

# Why We Are Truly a Nation

Because we rage inside
the old boundaries,
like a young girl leaving the Church,
scared of her parents.

Because we all dream of saving
the shaggy, dung-caked buffalo,
shielding the herd with our bodies.

Because grief unites us,
like the locked antlers of moose
who die on their knees in pairs.

# On Cape Cod a Child Is Stolen

Fog has sealed in the house
like a ship in a bottle.
All the people of the house
are dreaming of his future;
only the Puritans
and he aren't sleeping.
They watch him lie too long in bed,
the fog's moist nose at his ear.
Now the muzzle pokes his tiny mouth,
prying it open. They love him;
he's in danger; but it's too late.
His perfect body is still there
but clearly empty. The fog
rolls back to its own place
and the fishermen scrape back
from breakfast and go out to work.

# Driving All Night

My complicated past is an anthology,
a long line painted on the plains.
I feel like literary history
about to startle the professors.

But it's not true.

Days ahead, snow heaps up
in the mountains
like undelivered mail.
After driving all night
I guess what it's like
to fly over them.
For the first time you see
how close things are together,
how the foothills push up
just past where you quit
driving. Urgencies
sputter in the exaltation
of chill air.

       Your heart
begins to fall like snow
inside a paperweight.
Oh when in your long damn life,
I ask myself, when will
you seek not a truce,
but peace?

# Oh Yes

My hands, my fists, my small bells
of exact joy,
clappers cut out
because they have lied.

And your tongue:
like a burnt string
it holds its shape until
you try to lift it.

We're sewn into each other
like money in a miser's coat.
Don't cry. Your wounds are
beautiful if you'll love mine.

# Old Girlfriends

I thrust my impudent
cock into them
like a hand raised in class.

What they knew that I didn't learn
was not to ask:

one participates.

To say one is "in love"
says everything:
the tongue depressor breaks
into flame.

To say "one" is in love
means me, hero of all these poems,
in love as in a well
I am the water of.

# What You Need

Suppose you want to leave your life,
that old ring in the tub,
behind?

It closes cozily
as a clerk's hand,
a coin with fingers.

You hate it
the same way the drunken son
loves Mother.

You will need pain
heaving under you
like frost ruining the new road.

# Wehlener Sonnenuhr Auslese 1959

*for Dave Curry*

After each rain the workers
bring the eroded soil
back up the slope in baskets.
When the freezing ground heaves
rocks up, they are gathered,
shattered, the pieces
strewn among the vines.
The sun reflects from them.
In the Moselle the sun
is a broken bottle of light,
same color as the wine.
When you drink it,
you pass through your body
a beloved piece of earth.
You are like the worm,
except you know it.
A door in the earth opens
and you go in, as guest.

# Yes!

You come home loved and troubled,
tired,
and lay your body down before me
like new bread.
It is the same body I have always loved,
and in it your eyes shine
like light still traveling from a dead star.
I give you my love to use
and shake with fear you can't.
A sleep like a long swim
and dreams of things growing,
shuddering, wrenched,
giant kelp 100 ft. high in the ocean,
sage and yarrow,
the ferny lace of hair
around your cunt, marrow
in mending bones.
There is no way to stop growing.
Sleep is a simple faith.
I wake, wanting
the moist pull into you,
your face easing,
love growing in sweet violence.
And then you wake,
still tired, tentative
but languorous.
I know that love is life's best work.

# Sleek for the Long Flight

*(1972)*

# Directions

The new road runs into
the old road, turn
west when your ankles hurt.
The wind will be thinning itself
in the grass. Listen, those thuds
are bees drunk with plunder
falling from the minarets of flowers
like ripe prayers.
Follow the path
their bodies make. Faster.
The dirt in that wineglass
came from Chateau d'Yquem.
You're getting closer.
That pile of clothes
is where some women
enter the river. Hurry up.
The last hill is called
Sleep's Kneecap, nobody
remembers why.
This is where the wind turns
back. From the ridge
you can see the light.
It's more like a bright soot,
really, or the dust
a moth's wing leaves
on the thumb and forefinger.
This is where I turn
back—you go the rest of the way
by eating the light until
there is none and the next one
eats along the glow
of your extinguished hunger and turns
to the living.

# Sleeping Alone

*A man is a necessity.* A girl's mother says so by the way her hands come together after certain conversations, like a diary being closed.

But a boy's mother tells him *a woman is a luxury.* Maybe when he graduates his mother hugs him and forgets herself, she bites his earlobe! She remembers the hockey skates she gave him for Christmas when he was eight; the stiff flaps in back of the ankles resembled monks' cowls. The year before, the road froze over — they seemed to be what he should want.

Meanwhile the girl grows older, she hasn't been eight for ten years, her father is cruel to her mother. She'll always have a man, the way she likes to have in her room, even when visiting, a sandalwood box for her rings and coins, and a hand-painted mug showing two geese racing their reflections across a lake.

Maybe she will meet the boy, maybe not. The story does not depend on them. In a dark room a couple undress. She has always liked men's backs and holds on with her fingertips, like suction cups, turning one cheek up to him and staring through the dark across the rippled sheet. He breathes in her ear — some women like that. Or maybe they've loved each other for years and the lights are on. It doesn't matter; soon they will be sleeping.

Why do we say we *slept with* someone? The eyelids fall. It isn't *the one you love* or anyone else you recognize who says the only words you will remember from the dream. It must be the dream speaking, or the pope of all dreams speaking for the church. It says, *It's OK, we're only dying.*

# Driving Alongside the Housatonic River
# Alone on a Rainy April Night

I remember asking
where does my shadow go at night?
I thought it went home,
it grew so sleek at dusk.
They said, you just don't
notice it, the way you don't tell yourself
how to walk or hear
a noise that doesn't stop.
But one wrong wobble
in the socket and inside the knee
chalk is falling, school
is over.
As if the ground were a rung
suddenly gone from a ladder,
the self, the shoulders bunched
against the road's each bump, the penis
with its stupid grin,
the whole rank slum of cells
collapses.
I feel the steering wheel
tug a little, testing.
For as long as that takes
the car is a sack of kittens
weighed down by stones.
The headlights chase a dark ripple
across some birch trunks.
I know it's there, water
hurrying over the shadow of water.

# Another Beer

The first one was for the clock
and its one song
which is the song's name.

Then a beer for the scars in the table,
all healed in the shape of initials.

Then a beer for the thirst
and its one song we keep forgetting.

And a beer for the hands
we are keeping to ourselves.
The body's dogs, they lie
by the ashtray and thump
suddenly in their sleep.

And a beer for our reticence,
the true tongue, the one song,
the fire made of air.

Then a beer for the juke box.
I wish it had the recording
of a Marcel Marceau mime performance:
28 minutes of silence,
2 of applause.

And a beer for the phone booth.
In this confessional you can sit.
You sing it your one song.

And let's have a beer for whoever goes home
and sprawls, like the remaining sock,
in the drawer of his bed and repeats
the funny joke and pulls it
shut and sleeps.

And a beer for anyone
who can't tell the difference between
death and a good cry
with its one song.
None of us will rest enough.

The last beer is always for the road.
The road is what the car drinks
traveling on its tongue of light
all the way home.

# Night Driving

You follow into their dark tips
those two skewed tunnels of light.
Ahead of you, they seem to meet.
When you blink, it is the future.

# The Needle's Eye, the Lens

Here comes the blind thread to sew it shut.

# An Egg in the Corner of One Eye

I can only guess what it contains. I lean to the mirror like a teenager checking his complexion. Maybe it is sleep. Or a dream in which, like a bee or nursing mother or a radish, you eat to feed others. Or maybe it is a shard of light in the shape of an island from which dogs are leaping into the water, swimming toward a barking that only death can hear. On the eye's other shore life is upside-down. The dogs have swum for days to clamber up and, like an eye in its deathbed, shake out rays of light. Or maybe the light implodes. Or sinks into itself like a turned-off TV, the optic nerve subsiding like a snapped kitestring. I don't know. To open a tear is to kill whatever it was growing. I can't tell the difference between grief and joy. I tell myself that a tear is my death, leaking. In this way weeping resembles menstruation. The egg that will be fertilized never sees the light of day.

# The Cat

While you read
the sleepmoth begins
to circle your eyes
and then—
a hail of claws
lands the cat
in your lap.
The little motor
in his throat
is how a cat says
*Me.* He rasps the soft
file of his tongue
along the inside
of your wrist.
He licks himself.
He's building
a pebble of fur
in his stomach.
And now he pulls
his body in a circle
around the fire of sleep.

This is the wet
sweater with legs
that shakes in
from the rain,
split-ear the sex burglar,
Fish-breath, Wind-
minion, paw-poker
of dust
tumbleweeds,

the cat that kisses
with the wet
flame of his tongue
each of your eyelids
as if sealing
a letter.

One afternoon
napping under the light-
ladder
let down by the window,
there are two of them:
cat and cat-
shadow, sleep.

One night you lay your book
down like the clothes
your mother wanted
you to wear tomorrow.
You yawn.
The cat exhales a moon.
Opening a moon,
you dream of cats.
One of them strokes you
the wrong way. Still,
you sleep well.

This is the same cat
Plunder.
This is the old cat
Milk-whiskers.
This is the cat
eating one of its lives.
This is the first cat
Fire-fur.
This is the next cat
St. Sorrow.

This is the cat with its claws
furled, like sleep's flag.
This is the lust cat
trying to sleep with its shadow.
This is the only cat
I have ever loved.
This cat has written
in tongue-ink
the poem you are reading now,
the poem scratching
at the gate of silence,
the poem
that forgives
itself
for its used-up lives,
the poem
of the cat waking,
running a long shudder
through his body,
stretching again,
following the moist bell
of his nose
into the world
again.

# Talk

The body is never silent. Aristotle said that we can't hear the music of the spheres because it is the first thing that we hear, blood at the ear. Also the body is brewing its fluids. It is braiding the rope of food that moors us to the dead. Because it sniffles and farts, we love the unpredictable. Because breath goes in and out, there are two of each of us and they distrust each other. The body's reassuring slurps and creaks are like a dial tone: we can always call up the universe. And so we are always talking. My body and I sit up late, telling each other our troubles. And when two bodies are near each other, they begin talking in body-sonar. The art of conversation is not dead! Still, for long periods, it is comatose. For example, suppose my body doesn't get near enough to yours for a long time. It is disconsolate. Normally it talks to me all night: listening is how I sleep. Now it is truculent. It wants to speak directly to your body. The next voice you hear will be my body's. It sounds the same way blood sounds at your ear. It is saying *Ssshhh*, now that we, at last, are silent.

# La Tâche 1962

*for Michael Cuddihy*

Pulling the long cork, I shiver with a greed so pure it is curiosity. I feel like the long muscles in a sprinter's thighs when he's in the blocks, like a Monarch butterfly the second before it begins migrating to Venezuela for the winter—I feel as if I were about to seduce somebody famous. Pop. The first fumes swirl up. In a good year the Domaine de la Romanée-Conti gets maybe 20,000 bottles of La Tâche; this is number 4,189 for 1962. In the glass the color is intense as if from use or love, like a bookbinding burnished by palm oil. The bouquet billows the sail of the nose: it is a wind of loam and violets. "La tâche" means "the task." The word has implications of piecework; perhaps the vineyard workers were once paid by the chore rather than by the day. In a good year there would be no hail in September. Work every day. Finally, the first pressing of sleep. Stems, skins, a few spiders, yeast-bloom and dust-bloom on the skins. . . . Now the only work is waiting. On the tongue, under the tongue, with a slow breath drawn over it like a cloud's shadow—, the wine holds and lives by whatever it has learned from 3½ acres of earth. What I taste isn't the wine itself, but its secrets. I taste the secret of thirst, the longing of matter to be energy, the sloth of energy to lie down in the trenches of sleep, in the canals and fibres of the grape. The day breaks into cells living out their secrets. Marie agrees with me: this empty bottle number 4,189 of La Tâche 1962 held the best wine we have ever drunk. It is the emblem of what we never really taste or know, the silence all poems are unfaithful to. Michael, suppose the task is to look on until our lives have given themselves away? Amigo, Marie and I send you our love and this poem.

# Snow

The dog's spine, like a dolphin's,
sews a path
through the smaller drifts.
These graying roadside lumps,
like sheets waiting to be washed. . . .
You have to press 4,000 snowgrapes
for one bottle of this winter light.
A white moss girdles
every tree.
          All the erased
roads lead north, into the wind.
The house is a sack of sour breath
on the earth's back.
Glass drumskins
in the windows quiver.

I stare in a stupor of will,
fleck-faced, bearing my cow of a body
easily on the earth.
Intricate adjustments in my inner ears
and the gravitational habits of planets
keep me steady.
It's nothing personal, I know,
but so much basic work is being done for me
I ought to stop whining.

Sky shreds,
woods fade
like an old grainy photograph.

Slick white gearwheels mesh
and turn:
                which is what makes the hiss.
It is the suck and sigh
of shattered air
hoping to be ocean.
It is the glut of snow that I love.
A snowpelt
grows on the mailbox, the Volvo, the dog.
When I turn up
my eyes, my snow
rises to meet the snow.

# Sleep

Last cough,
lungcells six hours safe from cigarettes.
The testicles drone
in their hammocks,
making sperm.
Glut and waste
and then the beach invasion,
people
everywhere, the earth in its regular
whirl slurring to silence
like a record at the onset
of a power failure.
I'm burning ferns to heat my house.
I am
The Population Bomb, no,
not a thing but a process:
fire: fire.

Ashes and seeds.
Now in my drowse I want to spend,
spend before the end.
Sleep with a snowflake,
wake with a wet wife.
This is the dream in which the word "pride"
appears as a comet.
Its tail is the whole language
you tried as a child to learn.

Difficult and flashy dreams!
But they're all
allegory, like that comet.
You can turn your head fast
and make the light smear,
and you wake to watch it
staining the windows, good
stunned morning, people
everywhere, all of us
unraveling, it's so good
to be alive.

# Letter to Russell Banks

*Ithaca*
*January thaw 1971*

Dear Russ,
                    Another daughter! Old friend
you are indeed pillowed
by love of women. As I walk
all the woodlands for sale
near Ithaca, trolling for the land
that will lure me
down like a dowser's wand,
I feel the fist in all of us
opening. On the palm—
a tiny fist like a pink lettuce-head.
Our children are the only message
we can leave them.

Solstice, pivot of faded light.
But now it's ooze and spreading edges,
40° and down to 10° at night,
cars slurring lanes on the slick
morning roads, the day-long
drip from the eaves. The stiff
shriveled berries of the yew
burn free from the snow.
My greed for land swells
like a tick. Creek water leaks
to the surface.

Spiked by a slim maple:
a huge hornet's nest,
serene, a blank face
waiting to be minted.
Thinking of a new house means

redefining love.
Nobody knows how deep
we'll have to drill the well.

Stepping into woods, I think
of my ancestors and how Wales
and Norway are slivers in the globe.
I dwindle into the woods
and know why they were terrified.
Nobody knew Jamestown
stretched to the Pacific Ocean.
So you cut down a tree,
made a stake, beat it
into the earth and
hung on as a flag.
The wilderness was
too large then for us to love,
as is the city now.
Wilderness, here we come
again, ants dragging
a bulldozer, a sewer
like a gut straightened out.
Deep in the woods now
I spin suddenly to surprise
and see whatever follows me.
It is the memory of a tail,
the thrash of its absence.

*Fish-in-the-wrist,*
*cloud-in-the-mouth,*
*go home.*

I explain I'm looking for a home.

*Stone-in-the-throat,*
*fern-foot,*
*fire burns wherever it goes.*

All those dough-flecked hands
cupping one flame of solitude!
Mothers, girlfriends, wives
and daughters.
The spine like a lodgepole of fire.

                  yrs, burning outward,
                  Bill

# Sticks & Stones

*(1975)*

# The Portrait

Before the shutter blinks
the bored photographer can feel
the engaged couple stiffen—
lapse between a lightning bolt
and thunder. It's easy.
A train of light streaks into the tunnel
of his lens and comes out
changed. He loves his darkroom
trance, air in an inky lung.
And in the hall
outside: bell-shaped, its lipped rim
pressed to the ceiling, a cream-
colored glass lampshade
is rung by ricocheting moths.

# Mud Chokes No Eels

Sceptors and suitors hate competitors. Who may be
trusted with a houseful of millstones? When the shepherd
is angry with his sheep, he sends them a blind guide.
Imagine a wisdom better than grace. Time is a file that
wears and makes no noise. Imagine me living alone, watering
the German ivy and cleaning out the three-quart blue-and-
white-striped bowl and washing the Mouli grater & some knives
& forks & spoons & the big chipped mug I use for coffee &
a slotted spoon. Imagine me feeling sorry for myself.

Flight toward preferment will be but slow without some
golden feathers. The morning lumps along. Bells call others
to church, but go not themselves. Imagine an August day:
the fields steam bugs, dogs follow their tongues to the
nearest thirst. Fields have eyes, and hedges ears. Grass
creaks in the heat. Nature draws more than ten oxen, and
why not? Do large trees give more shade than fruit?
Outside this house, and outside your new apartment without
kitchen windows—who can imagine a kitchen without windows?—
the summer is going to seed and so are we, are we. Land
was never lost for want of an heir. Fall distills in the
trees. There's no more truth in the plot of a story than
gold in an owl's claws. Wisdom is just another failure of
love. Love sleeps in its own puddle. Imagine a better
reason for being where you are. I have a good cloak, but
it is in France.

# Beer after Tennis, 22 August 1972

The Palms is dank with air-conditioning and Dave and I
go in. On its high perch the TV shrills like a parrot. Steve
and Vicky are worried because Vicky's first husband, declared
legally dead, is back, and he's the one who gave the police
the evidence to clear Steve of that murder charge. Another
beer. Some laundry. Pinball. When you served from the west
side of the court the tossed ball grew black and disappeared
into the sun and you hit it where you guessed it would come out.
Another beer. Nixon gets out of a plane. 1,500 young people,
as the TV calls them, cheer and wave signs. Praising his
wife, he tells them, "If you want to get ahead in politics,
marry above yourself." On cue they chant, "We want Pat, we
want Pat." "You can't have her," he says. Farther down the
bar a young people pours his beer and stares at Nixon. He
turns toward us: "Hey man, is this *live?*" It's live. Dave
and I play three games of pinball. We walk out into the lowered
sun and the chilled sweat is on our bodies like a moss. I
let Dave off by Sonia's house and drive on home to feed my dog.
As the earth turns, the sun appears to fall.

# Bring the War Home

In its tenth year we realize
the war will always live with us,
some drooling Uncle Cockroach
who won't die.
Why should he? We don't want to.
He's our obvious secret,
an insect in amber,
a bad marriage the kids
won't believe we fought
for their sakes.
It's too late for them to take
their country back, its three-legged
dogs and seedlings and medical
techniques you couldn't learn
in three decades of peace.
They're ours — didn't we
save their lives?
And we are theirs.
Our guilt is the heroin of Vietnam,
the best smack on the streets.

# The Waste Carpet

*God pity the many who will die of soap foam.*
                    —*David Ignatow*

No day is right for the apocalypse,
if you ask
a housewife in Talking Rock, Georgia,
or maybe Hop River, Connecticut.
She is opening a plastic bag.
A grotesque parody of the primeval muck
starts oozing out. And behold
the plastic bag is magic,
there is no closing it.
Soap in unsoftened water, sewage, Masonite shavings,
a liquefied lifetime subscription to *The New York Times*
delivered all at once.
Empty body stockings, limp,
forlorn, like collapsed lungs.
A slithering sludge of face cream,
an army of Xerox copies
traveling on its stomach of interoffice memos,
toothpaste tubes as wrung as a widow's hands.
Also,
two hundred and one tons of crumpled bumpers
wrapped in claim reports,
liquid slag, coal dust, plastic trimmings,
industrial excrementa.
Lake Erie is returning our gifts.
At first she thought she had won something.
Now it slithers through the house,
out windows, down the street,
spreading everywhere but heading, mostly, west.
Maybe *heading* is the wrong word,
implying shape, and choice.

It took the shape of the land
it rippled across like the last blanket.
And it went west because the way lay open.

Outside Ravenswood, West Virginia,
abandoned cars shine in the sun like beetlebacks.
The amiable cars wait stilly in their pasture.
Three Edsels forage in the southeast corner,
a trio of ironical bishops.
There are Fords & Dodges,
a Mercury on blocks,
four Darts & a Pierce-Arrow,
a choir of silenced Chevrolets.
And, showing their absurd grills
and trademarks to a new westward expansion,
two Hudsons, a LaSalle, and a DeSoto.

I was hoping to describe the colors
of this industrial autumn —
rust, a faded purple like the skin
of a dusty Concord grape,
moss green, fern green, a deeper green
the diver sees beneath him when he reaches 30 feet —
but now they are all covered,
rolling and churning in the last accident,
bubbles in lava.

Behold
the poet must remember the words that will carve themselves
on his gravestone.
If you walk in the right cemetery,
that card catalogue of dirt, that grassy anthology,
you may read them:
*It is only art.*
A lifetime, muttering.

The Lamb's Head Inn at Lebanon,
the Little Miami River limbering

its length through Troy toward Cincinnati,
the Symphony Orchestra, the Wiedemann's Brewery,
the blue, indoors & smoky air
through which I watched
The Big O, Oscar Robertson,
turning his wheel of grace,
lofting a lifetime of basketballs.
First we lived on Glade Street, then
on Richwood Ave. I swear it.
And now all Cincinnati —
the hills above the river,
the lawn that sloped toward Richwood Ave.
like a valley of pleasant uncles,
the sultry river musk that slid
its compromising note
through my bedroom window —
all Cincinnati seethes. The vats
at Procter & Gamble cease their slick
congealing. The soap reverts to animal fat.
Up north, near Lebanon and Troy an Rosewood,
the corn I skulked in as a boy
lays back its ears like a shamed dog.
Hair along the hog's spine rises,
the Holstein pivots his massive head
at dusk toward where the barn was.
The spreading stain he sees is his new owner.

It is like being in a Catholic church
the night before Easter.
The statues stir under the heavy purple drapes.
The stiff gods we have made
so lovingly
ripple their stony muscles.
The slime crests toward the Mississippi.
Cairo, Natchez, New Orleans,
the litany of the new flood.

What we imagined was
the fire-storm.
Or, failing that, the glacier, or
we hoped we'd get off easy,
losing only California.
With the seismologists & mystics
we saw the last California ridge
crumble into the ocean
like Parmesan.
We would learn to love Nevada
and develop a taste for salt
in our water, our thirst
become a wound.

We were ready with elegies:

O California, sportswear
& defense contracts, gases that induce deference,
high school girls with their own cars,
we wanted to love you
without pain.

O California
when you were moored to us
like a splinter of melon bobbing among tankers
we knew the European tongue was cobblestone.
But now you are lost at sea,
your cargo of mudslides & vineyards
lost, the prints of the old movies
lost, the thick unlighted candles of the redwoods
snuffed in advance. On the ocean floor
they lie like hands of a broken clock.

We're all coming west
inexorably, bringing our ruinous
self-knowledge,
quoting Ecclesiastes.

We'll be there Friday, early,
your time.

Meanwhile
because this poem does not stop for lamentation
Kansas is stuck in unspeakable gluck,
in geological purge.
The jayhawk plummets in mid-flight,
drawn down by anklets of DDT.
Now we are about to lose our voices
we remember:
tomorrow is our echo.
O the old songs, the good days:
strip mining & civil disobedience,
sloppy scholarship, heart attacks.
Now the age of footnotes is ours.
So much for the Rockies,
so much for the rest.
Ibid, ibid, ibid, ibid, ibid.

While the rivers thickened
and fish rose like oil slicks
the students of water
stamped each fish with its death date.
Now we hear the sea rising
like a new vowel
in our throats.

## Sticks & Stones

Because I have lived by poetry
lines nag me lovingly.
Like these from Roethke's notebooks:
"I'm sick of women.  I want God"
and
"Does God *want* all this attention?"
Or Margaret Atwood's lines:
"you become slowly more public,
in a year there will be nothing left
of you but a megaphone."
Soon, will I be reciting these lines?
Will there be a party
after the reading?
Who will be there?
Moonrock, the anthologist.
A woman poet
afraid of living on her looks—
may she grow older.
There will be groupies—
may their pubic hair
clog the teeth of bad poets.
There will be the poet
whose marriage poems
are really about his writing students—
may his divorce poems
be better.
There will be the poet
overlooked by Moonrock—
may he turn in his sleep
like a lottery drum.
The Dark Prince will be there

in a dust-jacket,
sexual strip-miner and Dust
Midas, a love only
a mother could face.
Someone will know a cruel joke
so funny he'll tell it anyhow.
Will Twitch the Ironist be there?
Will the best young poet
in America be there?
Dervish will be there —
may his disciples
return to him
the gift of himself.
We don't need each other.
We need ceremonies of self-love
performed without witnesses.
We need to leave the party,
like a car starting across the fields.
It is time to be lost
again, weeping into the trenches
of our palms
until the hands are flooded
and the need begins to grow
like rice in a paddy
to hold something.
Then if I pick up a pen
and write a poem
I will want to read it to someone
and the poem will *be* the party
to honor whomever I read it to,
a fallen apple branch
cut into firewood,
cold milk in the morning,
a long walk at night.

# Rising and Falling
*(1979)*

# Spring Snow

Here comes the powdered milk I drank
as a child, and the money it saved.
Here come the papers I delivered,
the spotted dog in heat that followed me home

and the dogs that followed her.
Here comes a load of white laundry
from basketball practice, and sheets
with their watermarks of semen.

And here comes snow, a language
in which no word is ever repeated,
love is impossible, and remorse. . . .
Yet childhood doesn't end,

but accumulates, each memory
knit to the next, and the fields
become one field. If to die is to lose
all detail, then death is not

so distinguished, but a profusion
of detail, a last gossip, character
passed wholly into fate and fate
in flecks, like dust, like flour, like snow.

# Moving Again

At night the mountains look like huge
dim hens. In a few geological eras
new mountains may
shatter the earth's shell
and poke up like stone wings.
Each part must serve for a whole.
I bring my sons to the base
of the foothills and we go up.
From a scruff of ponderosa
pines we startle gaudy swerves
of magpies that settle in our rising
wake. Then there's a blooming
prickly pear. "Jesus, Dad, what's that?"
Willy asks. It's like a yellow tulip
grafted to a cactus: it's a beautiful
wound the cactus puts out
to bear fruit and be healed.
If I lived with my sons
all year I'd be less sentimental
about them. We go up
to the mesa top and look down
at our new hometown. The thin air
warps in the melting light
like the aura before a migraine.
The boys are tired. A tiny magpie
fluffs into a pine far below
and farther down in the valley
of child support and lights
people are opening drawers.
One of them finds a yellowing
patch of newsprint with a phone

number penciled on it
from Illinois, from before they moved, before
Nicky was born. Memory
is our root system.
"Verna," he says to himself
because his wife's in another room,
"whose number do you suppose this is?"

# Snow Leopards at the Denver Zoo

There are only a hundred or so
snow leopards alive, and three
of them here. Hours I watch them jump
down and jump up, water being
poured. Though if you fill a glass
fast with water, it rings high to the top,
noise of a nail driven true. Snow
leopards land without sound,
as if they were already extinct.

If I could, I'd sift them
from hand to hand, like a fire,
like a debt I can count but can't pay.
I'm glad I can't. If I tried to
take loss for a wife, and I do,
and keep her all the days of my life,
I'd have nothing to leave my children.
I save them whatever I can keep
and I pour it from hand to hand.

# The News

From each house on the street,
the blue light of the news.
Someone's dog whirps three times
and scuffs the leaves.
It's quiet, a school night.
The President and his helpers
live at one end of the news,
parents at the other.
The news for today
is tape recordings
of dry ice, sports
for today is weather.
Lights go back into the walls.
These might as well be
my neighbors. The news
uses us all to travel by.
I might as well be one
of their children, bees
sleeping the treaty of honey.
The news will find me soon
enough. I veer between
two of their houses
home through the woods.

## Strange Knees

It's one of the ways you see
yourself. Over the snow's blue skin
you go strictly, to honor the slag
of calcium in your knees,
to honor the way you say

Bad Knees, Bad Dog, Bad Luck.
Your sons love to hear how you
collapsed in the lobby
of Cinema II, a latch in your knee
not catching.

                It's true your knees
hurt all the time but your sons dote
wrongly on that fact. They make you Pain's
Firework. They want to know why
they love you and they eat your stories

up. You saved the cat. You're squeaking
home two miles over the moonwashed
snow because your car broke down.
The stories grow crooked inside
you and your knees grow bad.

# Living Among the Dead

*There is another world,*
*but it is in this one.*
        —*Paul Eluard*


First there were those who died
before I was born.
It was as if they had just left
and their shadows would
slip out after them
under the door so recently closed
the air in its path was still
swirling to rest.
Some of the furniture came from them,
I was told, and one day
I opened two chests
of drawers to learn what the dead kept.

But it was when I learned to read
that I began always
to live among the dead.
I remember Rapunzel,
the improved animals
in the *Just-So Stories,* and a flock
of birds that saved themselves
from a hunter by flying in place
in the shape of a tree,
their wings imitating the whisk
of wind in the leaves.

My sons and I are like some wine
the dead have already bottled.
They wish us well, but there is nothing
they can do for us.

Sebastian cries in his sleep,
I bring him into my bed,
talk to him, rub his back.
To help his sons live easily
among the dead is a father's great work.
Now Sebastian drifts, soon he'll sleep.
We can almost hear the dead
breathing. They sound like water
under a ship at sea.

To love the dead is easy.
They are final, perfect.
But to love a child
is sometimes to fail at love
while the dead look on
with their abstract sorrow.

To love a child is to turn
away from the patient dead.
It is to sleep carefully
in case he cries.

Later, when my sons are grown
among their own dead, I can
dive easily into sleep and loll
among the coral of my dreams
growing on themselves
until at the end
I almost never dream of anyone,
except my sons,
who is still alive.

# Left Hand Canyon

*for Richard Hugo*

The Rev. Royal Filkin preaches
tomorrow on why we are sad.
Brethren, Montana's a landscape
requiring faith: the visible
government arrives in trucks,
if you live out far enough.
If you live in town, the government's
gone, on errands, in trucks.

Let citizens go to meetings,
I'll stay home. I hate a parade.
By the time you get the trout
up through the tiny triangular
holes in the Coors cans, they're so
small you have to throw them back.
Glum miles we go
to Grandmother's house.

The earth out here doesn't bear us
up so much as it keeps us out,
an old trick of the beautiful.
Remember what Chief Left Hand said?
Never mind. Everything else
was taken from him,
let's leave his grief alone.
My Eastern friends ask me

how I like it in the West,
or God's country, as it's sometimes
called, though God, like a slumlord,
lives in the suburbs: Heaven.

And I don't live "in the West";
I live in this canyon among a few
other houses and abandoned
mines, vaccinations that didn't take.

# In Memory of the Utah Stars

Each of them must have terrified
his parents by being so big, obsessive
and exact so young, already gone
and leaving, like a big tipper,
that huge changeling's body in his place.
The prince of bone spurs and bad knees.

The year I first saw them play
Malone was a high school freshman,
already too big for any bed,
14, a natural resource.
You have to learn not to
apologize, a form of vanity.
You flare up in the lane, exotic
anywhere else. You roll the ball
off fingers twice as long as your
girlfriend's. Great touch for a big man,
says some jerk. Now they're defunct
and Moses Malone, boy wonder at 19,
rises at 20 from the St. Louis bench,
his pet of a body grown sullen
as fast as it grew up.

Something in you remembers every
time the ball left your fingertips
wrong and nothing the ball
can do in the air will change that.
You watch it set, stupid moon,
the way you watch yourself
in a recurring dream.
You never lose your touch

or forget how taxed bodies
go at the same pace they owe,
how brutally well the universe
works to be beautiful,
how we metabolize loss
as fast as we have to.

# Bud Powell, Paris, 1959

I'd never seen pain so bland.
Smack, though I didn't call it smack
in 1959, had eaten his technique.
His white-water right hand clattered
missing runs nobody else would think
to try, nor think to be outsmarted
by. Nobody played as well
as Powell, and neither did he,
stalled on his bench between sets,
stolid and vague, my hero,
his mocha skin souring gray.
Two bucks for a Scotch in this dump,
I thought, and I bought me
another. I was young and pain
rose to my ceiling, like warmth,
like a story that makes us come true
in the present. Each day's
melodrama in Powell's cells
bored and lulled him. Pain loves pain
and calls it company, and it is.

# Listening to Lester Young

*for Reg Saner*

It's 1958. Lester Young minces
out, spraddle-legged as if pain
were something he could step over
by raising his groin, and begins
to play. Soon he'll be dead.
It's all tone now and tone
slurring toward the center
of each note. The edges that used to be
exactly ragged as deckle
are already dead. His embouchure
is wobbly and he's so tired
from dying he quotes himself,
easy to remember the fingering.

It's 1958 and a jazz writer is coming home
from skating in Central Park. Who's that
ahead? It's Lester Young! *Hey Pres,*
he shouts and waves, letting his skates
clatter. *You dropped your shit,* Pres says.

It's 1976 and I'm listening
to Lester Young through stereo equipment
so good I can hear his breath rasp,
water from a dry pond—,
its bottom etched, like a palm,
with strange marks, a language
that was never born
and in which palmists therefore
can easily read the future.

# The Icehouse, Pointe au Baril, Ontario

Each vast block in its batter
of sawdust must have weighed
as much as I did. The sweat
we gathered running down
the path began to glaze.
We could see our breaths,
like comic strip balloons
but ragged, grey, opaque.

A warehouse of water on an island.
Once we arrived by seaplane:
the island looked like a green footprint.
Someone in a hurry saved time
by not sinking with each step.

In the icehouse I'd clear my name
on a block of ice and the dank film
of sawdust on my finger was as dense
as parts of grown-up conversation,
the rivalry of uncles and managing
money. The managers I knew
wore baseball caps and yelled.
As for money, I thought it was like food.
When blueberries were in season
we ate them all the time.

I always hoped to find a pickerel
in some block of ice
I was signing. Eyes frozen clear,
the tiny teeth like rasps on a file, the head
tapering to so fine a point it seemed

it could drill its way out. . . .
I'd smear the block clean with both hands cold
white under their gloves of sawdust.
*Look here,* I'd say clearly.

# The Mail

The star route man downshifts
his pale purple jeep called a Bronco
instead of a Rat or a Toucan.
The mailbox gets fed. Sharon mutters
out in her sweater, imploring
herself. What about? The wind,
water, the dead current of woodgrain
in the headboard of the bed.
She goes in to open the mail
which mainly says Read Me
I'm Here and See You
Tomorrow, (signed) little ripples
of ink. They make her want
to brush her hair and if it could
her hair would rise to the brush
like a happy pet. She stares
out the window. She could go anywhere.
Though the wind doesn't stop,
nor the light, to write a few words
beginning Dear Sharon, Dear Hair,
Dear Snowgrains Swirled Off The Roof,
Dear Window Pulling Me There.

# Taking the Train Home

1
Dusk grew on the window.
I'd listen for the click
of the seams in the rails
to come at the same speed
the telephone wires sagged
and then shot upward to the pole.
All night I slept between
the rails, a boy on a stretcher.
When I'd wake up outside
Chillicothe I felt like a fish.
Alfalfa and cows peered in
as I went by in my
aquarium, my night
in glass. Dawn flew against
my window the same way
a fly swarms by itself
against the heat of a bare
light bulb, like a heart attack.
I'd be home soon, 7:15,
all out for Cincinnati.

2
It's Sunday and I'm only four
and my grandparents are taking
me to Sharonville, to the roundhouse.
Pop drives. The part in the white crest
of his hair is like a compass needle.
Non sings. From the back seat

I lean between them, I can
feel the soot, the cinders
like black popcorn under my feet.
The roundhouse ceiling is charred
by sparks, and grime
smears its highest windows.
Coalcars smolder on sidings
while the engine turns
away from its arrival.

I was going to live in a roundhouse
when I grew up, a lighthouse.
Every morning the moon
would steam in over the sea
and turn around.
The table would be set for breakfast
before I went to bed,
my little tower of pills
beside the juice glass.
My hair would be white, like Pop's,
and by its light the ships,
long pods of sleep and fuel oil,
coffee beans, brooms
with real straw,
by the light of my hair
ships would sleep into port
and germinate.


3
In my dream I'm only four
again, Pop is alive.
He walks slowly — emphysema.
I've eaten something
metallic, something
I don't understand.

I circle away from him
to vomit among roadside weeds.
I force it up.
It's like gruel, with roofing nails
for lumps.
I love this dying man.
I look up and he bobs over a wave
in the road, he's swimming
out to sea. I begin
following but my legs are too short,
death is my father,
this is my body
which will fall apart.
I'm sleeping on the ocean.
I'm asleep on a train
outside Red Lion, Ohio.
I don't know; I can't tell,
but it seems to me
that if I could watch my body sleep
it would glow,
growing its antibodies
to eternal life,
growing the lives we give away
when we wake.

# Waking at Dusk from a Nap

In the years that pass through
an afternoon's dream, like tape
at Fast Forward, there are
syllables, somehow, in the waterfall,
and in the dream I hear them each
clearly, a classroom
of children reciting their names.
I am not in the dream; it's as if I am
the dream, in which such distinctions
go without saying. And in which
a confusion I may soon have—did I
wake at dawn or dusk?—seems
anticipated: a strand of stars
goes by, like elephants spliced
trunk-to-tail in children's books
or ivory carvings, and the dream won't say
if they're through for the night
or amiably headed for work.

And the dream—and once, I remember,
it seemed I was the dream—
the dream tilts up to pour me out.

For an instant when I wake
there's a whir, perhaps of props
and stagehands, and a laggard star
scrambles over the transom.
The grainy world with its sworls
and lesions, its puckering dusk light,
its dimming patina, its used and casual
beauty, reassembles itself exactly.

And I climb down from the bed, gather
my spilled book from the floor,
and watch the lights come on
in the valley, like bright type
being set in another language.

# In Memory of W. H. Auden

1

His heart made a last fist.
The language has used him
well and passed him through.
We get what he collected.
The magpie shines, burns
in the face of the polished stone.

2

His was a mind alive by a pure greed
for reading, for the book
which "is a mirror,"
as Lichtenberg said: "if an ass
peers into it, you can't expect
an apostle to look out."

It was a mediating mind.
There were the crowds like fields of waving wheat
and there was the Rilkean fire
he didn't like
at the bottom of the night.
He loomed back and forth.
The space shrank.
The dogs of Europe wolved
about the house,
darks defining a campfire.

3

My friend said Auden died
because his face
invaded his body.
Under the joke is a myth —
we invent our faces:
the best suffer most and it shows.
But what about the face
crumpled by a drunk's Buick?
Or Auden's
face in its fugue of photographs
so suddenly resolved?
It isn't suffering that eats us.


4

They were not painting about suffering,
the Old Masters. Not the human heart but
Brueghel turns the plowman away
for compositional reasons
and smooths the waters for a ship he made
expensive and delicate.
The sun is implied by how
the sure hand makes the light fall
as long as we watch the painting.
The sure hand is cruel.

# Nurse Sharks

Since most sharks have no flotation bladders and must swim
to keep from sinking, they like to sleep in underwater caves,
wedged between reef-ledges, or in water so shallow
that their dorsal fins cut up from the surf.
Once I woke a nurse shark (so named because it was
thought to protect its young by taking them
into its mouth). It shied from the bubbles I gave up
but sniffed the glint the murky light made on my regulator.

My first shark at last. I clenched
every pore I could. A shark's sense of smell
is so acute and indiscriminate that a shark crossing
the path of its own wound is rapt.
Once a shark got caught, ripped open by the hook.
The fisherman threw it back after it flopped
fifteen minutes on deck, then caught it again
on a hook baited with its own guts.

Except for the rapacious great white
who often bites first, sharks usually nudge
what they might eat. They're scavengers and like
food to be dead or dying. Move to show you're alive
but not so much as to cause panic: that's what the books
advise. The nurse shark nibbled at my regulator
once, a florid angelfish swam by, the shark
veered off as if it were bored. Its nubbled skin
scraped my kneecap, no blood
but the rasped kneecap pink for a week.

Another year I swam past a wallow of nurse sharks asleep
in three feet of water, their wedge-shaped heads lax

on each other's backs. One of them slowly thrashed
its tail as if it were keeping its balance in the thicket
of sharks sleeping like pick-up sticks. Its tail sent
a small current over me, a wet wind.
I swirled around a stand of coral and swam
fast to shore, startling the sharks to a waking frenzy:
moil, water opaque with churned-up sand,
grey flames burning out to sea. Last time I go diving
alone, I promised myself, though I lied.

# Long

*for Stanley Plumly*

It's about to be too late.
Every shred of the usual weather
is precious and sexual as it goes,
the way the links of a fugue become
one another's strict abandonments.

As for the future, it will not swerve.
Fire sleeps in the tree. Which tree?
Fire sleeps without dreaming and cannot
say. If we call the future's name
it becomes our name, by echo.

And from the dead, not even
a plea that we leave them
alone, each dead locked
in its dead name. If the dead complained,
they would say we summon them poorly,

dull music and thin wine, nor love
enough for the many we make,
much less for the melted dead
in their boxes. Above them
we talk big, since the place is vast

and bland if we tire of looking closely,
washed bland by light from what light
lets us see, our study,
the scripture of matter,
our long narcosis of parting.

# Flood

*(1982)*

# New

The long path sap sludges up
through an iris, is it new
each spring? And what would
an iris care for novelty?
Urgent in tatters, it wants
to wrest what routine it can
from the ceaseless shifts
of weather, from the scrounge
it feeds on to grow beautiful
and bigger: last week the space
about to be rumpled
by iris petals was only air
through which a rabbit leapt,
a volley of heartbeats hardly
contained by fur, and then the clay-
colored spaniel in pursuit
and the effortless air
rejoining itself whole.

# Cows Grazing at Sunrise

What the sun gives us,
the air it passes through aspires
to take back, and the day's long
bidding begins, itself a sort
of heat. Up goes the warm air
and down comes the cold.
In the cows' several bellies the bicker
of use is loud. Their dense heads
spill shadows thirty feet long,
heads that weigh as much as my grown
children, who can crack my heart:
the right tool makes any job
easy. And don't the cows know it,
and the dewy, fermenting grass?
And isn't the past inevitable,
now that we call the little
we remember of it "the past"?

# Housework

How precise it seems, like a dollhouse,
and look: the tiniest socks ever knit
are crumpled on a chair in your bedroom.
And how still, like the air inside a church
or basketball. How you could have lived
your boyhood here is hard to know,

unless the blandishing lilacs
and slant rain stippling the lamplight
sustained you, and the friendship of dogs,
and the secrecy that flourishes in vacant lots.
For who would sleep, like a cat in a drawer,
in this house memory is always dusting,

unless it be you? I'd hear you on the stairs,
an avalanche of sneakers, and then the sift
of your absence and then I'd begin to rub
the house like a lantern until you came back
and grew up to be me, wondering how to sleep
in this lie of memory unless it be made clean.

# Bystanders

When it snowed hard, cars failed
at the hairpin turn above the house.
They'd slur off line and drift
to a ditch — or creep back down,
the driver squinting out from a half-
open door, his hindsight glazed
by snow on the rear window
and cold breath on the mirrors.
Soon he'd be at the house to use
the phone and peer a few feet out
the kitchen window at the black
night and insulating snow.
Those were the uphill cars. One night
a clump of them had gathered
at the turn and I'd gone out
to make my usual remark —
something smug about pride disguised
as something about machines and snow —
and to be in a clump myself. Then
over the hillbrow one mile up the road
came two pale headlights and the whine
of a car doing fifty downhill through
four tufted inches of snow atop a thin
sheet of new ice. That shut us up,
and we turned in thrall, like grass
in wind, to watch the car and all
its people die. Their only chance
would be never to brake, but to let
the force of their folly carry them, as if
it were a law of physics, where it would,
and since the hill was straight until

the hairpin turn, they might make it
that far, and so we unclumped fast
from the turn and its scatter of abandoned cars;
and down the hill it came, the accident.
How beautifully shaped it was, like an arrow,
this violent privation and story
I would have, and it was only beginning.
It must have been going seventy when it
somehow insinuated through the cars
we'd got as far away from as we could,
and it left the road where the road left
a straight downhill line. Halfway
down the Morgans' boulder- and stump-
strewn meadow it clanged and yawed,
one door flew open like a wing, and then
it rolled and tossed in the surf of its last
momentum, and there was no noise from it.
The many I'd imagined in the car were only one.
A woman wiped blood from his crushed
face with a Tampax, though he was dead,
and we stood in the field and stuttered.
Back at the turn two collies barked
at the snowplow with its blue light
turning mildly, at the wrecker, at the police
to whom we told our names and what we saw.
So we began to ravel from the stunned
calm single thing we had become
by not dying, and the county cleared
the turn and everyone went home, and, while
the plow dragged up the slick hill the staunch
clank of its chains, the county cleared the field.

# Twins

*One may be a blameless*
*bachelor, and it is but a*
*step to Congreve.*
　　　　　—*Marianne Moore*


When I was eleven and they
were twenty-two, I fell in love
with twins: that's how I thought
of them, in sum, five run-on
syllables, Connie-and-Bonnie.
They were so resolutely given
as a pair—like father-and-
mother—I never thought to prefer one,
warm in her matching bed
like half an English muffin
in a toaster, though Bonnie
was blonde, lithe, walleyed,
angular, and fey. And Connie
was brunette, shiny-eyed, and
shy, as most true flirts
describe themselves, over and over.

And shouldn't love be an exclusive
passion? To fall in love with twins
made me unfaithful in advance?
It made me paralyzed, or I made
it—my love doubled forever
into mathematical heaven—paralysis.
Frocks rhyme and names confuse
and the world is thicker with sad
futures than lost pasts. And I,
who hoarded names like marbles,
how could I say what I knew?

Indeed, how can I say it now?
I knew the two meanings of *cleave*.
I looked into those eyes I loved,
two brown, two blue, and shut my own
(grey) from any light but mine
and walked straight home and kissed
my parents equally and climbed my growing
body's staircase to the very tip of sleep.

# Our Strange and Lovable Weather

*for Daniel Halpern*

First frost, and on the windows snow
is visible in embryo,
though Seattle has only one
snow a winter. Mostly we have
cool rain in fog, in drizzle, in mist
and sometimes in fat, candid drops
that lubricate our long, slow springs.
But I'm way ahead of myself.
From behind windows one season
is another. You have to go
out to feel if this is winter
gathering or giving itself up,
though whichever it may be, soon
enough turmoil under leafmold
begins, and the bulbs swell, and up
the longings of themselves spring's first
flowers shinny. February.
Here you can fill in the bad jokes
about weather and change, about
mixed feelings, about time, about
not wanting to die, and by the time
you've run round their circumference
the year has turned to May, and night
drags its feet home slow and dusty
as a schoolboy. But soon it's June,
usually rainy here, then summer
arrives in earnest, as we say,
with its long, flat light pulling
like an anchor against the sun.
How can the year have gone so fast?
Already the cool nights tuned

so perfectly to deep sleep admit
a few slivers of cold, then swatches,
and then they meet and are patterns.
First frost once again, we think.
Time to clear the clog of wet leaves
from the gutters, time to turn off
the water to the outside faucets.
And time to think how what we know
about our lives from watching this
is true enough to live them by,
though anyplace lies about its weather,
just as we lie about our childhoods,
and for the same reason: we can't
say surely what we've undergone,
and need to know, and need to know.

# Descriptive Passages

*Your hair is drunk again,*
someone explains to me.
And it's not only my hair:
no matter how rack-natty
my clothes were, they're rum-
pled on my body, dressed up
like a child performing
for its parents' guests.
How much of childhood
is spent on tiptoe! Clean up,
wise up, speak up, wake up
and act your age. But also one
is uppity: something's gone
to his head, a bubble
in the bloodstream, a scratch
in the record, a bad habit.

No theory can explain
personality, which expands
to include, if it can, all
its contradictory urges.
It's so hard to think about
this fact that we don't:
we use crude code. *The one*
*with the limp, with big tits,*
*with the drunk hair.* And we love
so much to be loved —
or failing that, remembered —
that we limp a little, and thrust
out our chests. On me it looks
good, as the hunchback said.

Use description carefully.
For example, today as I
glower out at morning fog
I can feel the fatigue
of matter, how glum a job
endurance is. The gulls
over Lake Union look heavy
and disconsolate, like office life.
Is this all there is, I could ask,
secretly excited
because if it is I've saved
myself so much response
and responsibility.

It's harder than we think
to name our children, but how
can we be accurate?
They'll find stories to live by.
I envision my children
sitting loosely in middle age.
I give them good wine to talk by,
I've lit them a fire if it's cold.
I can't leave them alone, I think
from the grave: a father's work
is never done. One son turns
to the other and says, *You know
how I always think of him?
I remember his drunk hair.*
There's a pause. It's harder
than we think to name
our emotions. *There were those
sentimental poems he wrote
about us, and his drunk hair,*
the other son says, proud
for the intimate talk and sad
for how little such talk says,
*though it wasn't drunk that often.*

# Good Company

At dinner we discuss marriage.
Three men, three women (one couple
among us), all six of us wary.
"I use it to frighten myself."
Our true subject is loneliness.
We've been divorced 1.5 times
per heart. "The trick the last half
of our lives is to get our work done."
The golfer we saw from the car
this afternoon, his angered
face in bloom with blood, lashed
his strict ball for going where he'd hit it.
We watched him turn from a worse shot
yet and give us a look like our own,
and on we dawdled through
the afternoon toward dinner,
here. Here means the married
couple's house, of course.
The rest of us use so much time
being alone we don't entertain much.
The wind loops and subsides.
"What a fine night to sleep!"
Upstairs a book falls off a shelf.
We'll be sitting here ages hence:
the scent of lawns, good company, Sancerre,
fitful breezes suddenly earnest.
"What sense does marriage make now?
Both people want jobs, the sad
pleasures of travel, and also
want homes. They don't want dark houses
or to live with cats. They have lives

waiting up for them at home.
Take me, I must read half an hour
of Horace before I can sleep."
The conversation luffs. The last
bottle of wine was probably too much
but God we're happy here.
"My husband stopped the papers
and flea-bathed the dog
before he left." One of us has a friend
whose analyst died in mid-session,
non-directive to the end.
Now we're drifting off to our nine lives
and more. Melodramatic wind,
bright moon, dishes to do, a last
little puddle of brandy or not,
and the cars amble home:
the door, the stairs, the sheets
aglow with reticence and moonlight,
and the bed full to its blank brim
with the violent poise of dreams.

# School Figures

*for Susan*

It's best to work before dawn:
fresh ice, its surface silvered
and opaque, and you scritch out
onto the milky ice, not avid
for grammar, too sleepy for speech.
It's not that you're marking time;
you're melting it grainy under
your runners. Each time you sweep

in your half-sleep around the figure
    eight, your blades are duller
and record how far you've slid
from your margin of error, zero.
That's why you skate it backwards.
It's where you've been you have to go
again, alert enough to numb
every muscle memory but one.

So much learning is forgetting
the many mistakes for the few
lines clear of the flourishes
you thought were style, but were
only personality, indelible as
it seemed. Who but you could
forge those stern exclusions? Where
the line of concentration crosses

itself, cutting and tying its knot
both, there learning and forgetting
are one attention, and are the thrall
that pulls you stiff-ankled over

the ice before dawn, turning
over your shoulder as if you could
skate back into your first
path and get it right for once.

# Pissing off the Back of the Boat
# into the Nivernais Canal

It's so cold my cock is furled
like a nutmeat and cold,
for all its warm aspirations
and traffic of urine. 37
years old and it takes me a second
to find it, the poor pink slug,
so far from the brash volunteer
of the boudoir. I arc a few
finishing stutters into the water.
Already they're converted,
opaque and chill. How com-
modious the dark universe is,
and companionable the stars.
How drunk I am. I shake
my shriveled nozzle and three
drops lurk out like syllables
from before there were languages. Snug
in my pants it will leak a whole sentence
in Latin. How like a lock-keeper's
life a penis biography would be,
bucolic and dull. What the penis
knows of sex is only arithmetic.
The tongue can kiss and tell.
But the imagination has,
as usual, most of the fun.
It makes discriminations,
bad jokes. It knows itself
to be tragic and thereby silly.
And it can tell a dull story well,
drop by reluctant drop.

What it can't do is be a body
nor survive time's acid work
on the body it enlivens,
I think as I try not to pitch
my wine-dulled body and wary
imagination with it into the inky
canal by the small force
of tugging my zipper up.
How much damage to themselves
the body and imagination
can absorb, I think as I drizzle
to sleep, and how much
the imagination makes
of its body of work
a place to recover itself.

# The Penalty for Bigamy Is Two Wives

I don't understand how Janis Joplin did it, how she made her voice break out like that in hives of feeling. I have a friend who writes poems who says he really wants to be a rock star—the high-heeled boots, the hand-held mike, the glare of underpants in the front row, the whole package. He says he likes the way music throws you back into your body, like organic food or heroin. But when he sings it is sleek and abstract except for the pain, like the silhouette of a dog baying at the moon, almost liver-shaped, a bell hung from a rope of its own pure yearning. Naturally his life is exciting, but sometimes I think he can't tell the difference between salvation and death. When I listen to my Janis Joplin records I think of him. Once I got drunk & sloppy and told him I feared artists always had more fun and more death, too, and how I had these strong feelings but nothing to do with them and he said *Don't worry I'd trade my onion collection for a good cry, wouldn't you?* I didn't really understand but poetry is how you feel so I lie back and listen to Janis's dead voice run up and down my body like a fire that has learned to live on itself and I think *Here it comes, Grief's beautiful blow job.* I think about the painter who was said to paint with his penis and I imagine one of his portraits letting down a local rain of hair around his penis now too stiff to paint with, as if her diligent silence meant to say *You loved me enough to make me, when will I see you next?* Janis, I don't care what anybody thinks or writes, I don't care if my friend who writes poems is a beautiful fake, like a planetarium ceiling, I want to hold my life in my arms as easily as my body will hold forever the silence for which the mouth slowly opens.

# Bmp Bmp

*for James McGarrell*

Lugubriously enough they're playing
*Yes We Have No Bananas* at deadpan
half-tempo, and Bechet's beginning
to climb like a fakir's snake,
as if that boulevard-broad vibrato
of his could claim space in the air,
out of the low register. Here comes
a spurious growl from the trombone,
and here comes a flutter of tourist
barrelhouse from the pianist's left hand.
Life is fun when you're good at something
good. Soon they'll do the *Tin Roof Blues*
and use their 246 years
of habit and convention hard.
Now they're headed out and everyone
stops to let Bechet inveigle his way
through eight bars unaccompanied
and then they'll doo dah doo dah doo
bmp bmp. Bechet's in mid-surge as usual
by his first note, which he holds, wobbles
and then pinches off to a staccato spat
with the melody. For a moment this stupid,
lumpy and cynically composed little money-
magnet of a song is played poor and bare
as it is, then he begins to urge it out
from itself. First a shimmering gulp
from the tubular waters of the soprano sax,
in Bechet's mouth the most metallic
woodwind and the most fluid, and then
with that dank air and airborne tone
he punches three quarter-notes

that don't appear in the song but should.
From the last of them he seems to droop,
the way in World War II movies
planes leaving the decks of aircraft carriers
would dip off the lip, then catch the right
resistance from wet air and strain up,
except he's playing against the regular disasters
of the melody his love for flight and flight's
need for gravity. And then he's up, loop
and slur and spiral, and a long, drifting note
at the top, from which, like a child decided
to come home before he's called, he begins to drift
back down, insouciant and exact, and ambles
in the door of the joyous and tacky chorus
just on time for the band to leave together,
headed for the *Tin Roof Blues*.

# Nabokov's Death

The solid shimmer of his prose
made English lucky that he wrote

plain English butterflies
and guns could read,

if they were fervent readers.
He loved desire. *Ada* could be

pronounced *Ah, Da!* — one
of those interlingual puns

he left, like goofy love notes,
throughout the startled house.

And yet we'll hold to our grief,
stern against grace, because we love

a broken heart, "the little madman
in his padded cell," as Nabokov

once described a fetus. For grief
is a species of prestige, if we mourn

the great, and a kind of power,
as if we had invented what we love

because it completes us. But
our love isn't acid: things deliquesce

on their own. How well he knew that,
who loved the art that reveals art

and all its shabby magic. The duelists
crumple their papier-mâché pistols.

The stage dead rise from the dead.
The world of loss is replete.

# On the Porch at the Frost Place, Franconia, NH

*for Stanley Plumly*

So here the great man stood,
fermenting malice and poems
we have to be nearly as fierce
against ourselves as he
not to misread by their disguises.
Blue in dawn haze, the tamarack
across the road is new since Frost
and thirty feet tall already.
No doubt he liked to scorch off
morning fog by simply staring through it
long enough so that what he saw
grew visible. "Watching the dragon
come out of the Notch," his children
used to call it. And no wonder
he chose a climate whose winter
and house whose isolation could be
stern enough to his wrath and pity
as to make them seem survival skills
he'd learned on the job, farming
fifty acres of pasture and woods.
For cash crops he had sweat and doubt
and moralizing rage, those staples
of the barter system. And these swift
and aching summers, like the blackberries
I've been poaching down the road
from the house where no one's home —
acid at first and each little globe
of the berry too taut and distinct
from the others, then they swell to hold
the riot of their juices and briefly
the fat berries are perfected to my taste,

and then they begin to leak and blob
and under their crescendo of sugar
I can taste how they make it through winter. . . .
By the time I'm back from a last,
six-berry raid, it's almost dusk,
and more and more mosquitoes
will race around my ear their tiny engines,
the speedboats of the insect world.
I won't be longer on the porch
than it takes to look out once
and see what I've taught myself
in two months here to discern:
night restoring its opacities,
though for an instant as intense
and evanescent as waking from a dream
of eating blackberries and almost
being able to remember it, I think
I see the parts — haze, dusk, light
broken into grains, fatigue,
the mineral dark of the White Mountains,
the wavering shadows steadying themselves —
separate, then joined, then seamless:
the way, in fact, Frost's great poems,
like all great poems, conceal
what they merely know, to be
predicaments. However long
it took to watch what I thought
I saw, it was dark when I was done,
everywhere and on the porch,
and since nothing stopped
my sight, I let it go.

# Uncollected Poems
*(1967–1981)*

# The Cloud

Here I am again,
fleet and green —
something that has left the shrubs
bleached, but in the old shapes,
some vegetable force
noticed only by its absence —
malingering through the house.

I rub my back on the ceiling
like smoke from the crushed cigarette
of a lover
escaped just in time:
the husband is coming
downstairs: a tennis ball,
a one-drop waterfall.
He has been wakened
from dreaming of love.

I hide in the shower.
This is fun! This is better
than rocking like a chair
someone has leapt up from,
rocking on my knees,
a nauseous monk,
the body shaken and sick
from dreaming of love,

my mind a thicket I peer from
watching my body vomit —
every nerve, every cilium
flapping free of its snapped tether.

I am a little fist
of shower mist,
a snarl in the dank air.

When it is safe I come out,
pale, bereft.
I want to tarnish the silverware,
to sleep in a drawer
forever, a tacky gift
dreaming of love.

I want to grow on the mirrors —
a mossy breath,
a life without a body
shaken and sick,
a life no larger than the smear
of structured slime, the microbe
that will kill me
dreaming of love.

I'm going to send you this poem
when I've finished it, it will
embarrass you
dreaming of love,
of the beach from which the cloud parade
is always starting
outward.
If the dream is inland,
the beach is a bed,
your body shaken and sick
of its dreaming of love,
the pale men stepping off the side
like suicidal pillows.
They have taken the wrong turn
for the Temple.
Perhaps you gave the directions,
dreaming of love,
your body shaken and sick

of its pale flags
nobody could see in a mist?
Where is the cloud flotilla?
It is carrying food to the fat ones.

Meanwhile in the kitchen
my tryst with the teakettle
had failed.
I'm oozing upstairs, I'm
like a beer growing a smaller head.
Here on this bed
I've dreamed of the love of one woman
at a time,
not caring who.
My body curled to sleep, a statue
of a snake.
There are no straight lines in nature.
If I writhed,
chances are
I was dreaming of love.

Then I would wake
to the trill in the forsythia,
the birds blunt in their needs.
Nothing in nature repeats.

So I rose —
a new noise
from a dropped tambourine.
And then I went to bed some more
and here I am
floating above my body,
a threatening rain
dreaming of love.

Who wants to hover long?
Those pale plants are my fault.
The ground is to fall down on

dreaming of love,
the body shaken and sick.

Wherever you are
dreaming of love,
good night.
The ferns of blood and light
knit shut my eyes,
coals in a later life.
Ashes to ashes, breath to breath.

Then I will go
down for breakfast
in a substantial dew.
Shredded wheat!
This must be how the medium feels
when his astral body comes
home after the séance —
foolish, whole.
Perhaps I am a fraud
dreaming of love,
my body shaken and sick.

The cold milk beads its glass.
The shrubs gleam green.
Dust in the lit air swirls.
I broke from my bed
like a pheasant.
I'm leaving myself off the hook
all day, you'll have to come over.
This is like the light before a tornado,
and it is only a new morning —
the raveled wheat reknit in its bowl,
the milk staring
from its faceted glass like a white bee,
the smooth udder of the sun
hung over my head

and yours, wherever you are.
I feel like a new tree,
a cloud with a stem
sunk in the earth of the body's
dream about the body
shaken and sick
dreaming of love.

# Eternally Undismayed Are the Poolshooters

*for Robert Peterson*

A slow circular flail of fan
not moving the still air.
Shee-it. Slap of pool balls. Hot.
Arms sag from sweat-stained sockets,
drenched tendrils.

"It's so hot at my place
you can hear the paint crack."

Everything's slick with a soft sweaty grit.
In the parking lot
a sponge-tongued beagle
spurns a dirty puddle
shaped like a woman's foot,
crumples into the shade
beneath a Buick, sleeps.

She loved heat.
On the beach for hours
like a snake, then daintily
to the water, foamtoes,
one deep breast-heaving breath
and in.

"104 out there. Too hot to fuck.
I once loved a woman left me
on a day like this."
We woke marbled with sweat.
"Those days I was working straight commission,
I could sell a truss to a trout.
I said, my love

let's buy an air conditioner.
She put my shirt on, then her slacks."
Like a bride aiming her bouquet
at a tubby friend, she tossed me
her underpants and left.
"I haven't seen her since."

Each ball slides for no reason
where it wants,
glasses of beer warm up to room
temperature (about 78°)
at the same pace
the balls click quietly
like tumblers in a lock.
Freddie brings the paper in,
hangs around, goes back out.
Nothing from the poolshooters,
faces of camels
working their gums
among the smoke rings.

# The Drunken Baker

Those pale fish, his hands —
he never thinks of them: what good
are married daughters?

Three days he's been like this.
They shape his every
loaf of breath.

# Leaving the Cleveland Airport

*for Robert & Tomas*

    In another language strange things happen. A razor can be a
rocket. The stewardesses murmur up and down the aisle like a
translator caught between languages, silences leaking from his hands
as he hurries. Or it could be something that those of us who travel
too much are trying to bring home: a swamp-bubble, a vowel from
the shadow language that is in the names of our wives and children,
something rising under the earth's skin like a sun of dirt and stone
and artifacts buried with the dead, and cave-water over which the
shadows of bats—who cannot see them—have written for centuries
their pure language without readers.

# Dancing to Reggae Music

The night, with its close breath
of sawdust and overproof rum,
its clatter of waxy leaves above
this scuff of earth we print
and erase — the night pours
over us its star-spotted syrup
of wakefulness. I love the halt
and stutter both, and the lyrics
with their exultant certainties
about politics and religion:
*I want to disturb my neighbor*
*'cause I'm feeling so right.*

Somebody's lit a spliff, I can tell
by the dense caramel of ganja smoke.
There are trances of paying
attention, and trances of giving
it up, which is where the blue-
grey ganja smoke will go, slowly,
it's so thick and layered,
and where the scent of dancing
will go, a little acrid the way
an armpit is after orgasm,
as if acrid meant truculent
to come back to our common life
after the trances of the self

we use each other for.
How easy it is to dance about
the self, and easy to confuse
it with the constellate body.

If they were the same, we couldn't
move, much less dance the night
away that's leaving us anyhow.
It too will go up, pushed back
by the salt light of dawn coming
from the ocean. And up is where
we go from here, after a detour
through dust. So long, politics
and religion. Hello, stars.

# Gossip

That year they said I was miserable, and it became an epithet, a destiny, an excuse.

They thought me miserable because they couldn't imagine themselves behaving so badly out of weakness or choice, but only if they were overcome by a superior force, like gravity or misery. They were wrong. I behaved badly on my own, and they can do it, too.

It was a sort of kindness, their myth of my misery: presently I'd be the real and better me. And it was a sort of malice: The Big Cheese is all parings.

But I was not miserable. The more the theory grew among them the more I grew secret—almost without effort, for they had given me an identity through which I couldn't be seen. And I grew happy.

And so it came to seem to me that they must be, because of their common error, miserable. Though I don't suppose they know it, and I won't say a word about it. I hate gossip.

# Iowa City to Boulder

I take most of the drive by night.
It's cool and in the dark my lapsed
inspection can't be seen.
I sing and make myself promises.

By dawn on the high plains
I'm driving tired and cagey.
Red-winged blackbirds
on the mileposts, like candle flames,
flare their wings for balance
in the blasts of truck wakes.

The dust of not sleeping
drifts in my mouth, and five or six
miles slur by uncounted.
I say I hate long-distance

drives but I love them.
The flat light stains the foothills
pale and I speed up the canyon
to sleep until the little lull
the insects take at dusk before
they say their names all night in the loud field.

# Lions in the Cincinnati Zoo

Compared to their bodies,
peeling in swatches
like old wallpaper, their pug
faces are too big and bland,
blank for some emotion
no zoo can induce.

In the wild their bloat outlopes
hunger, but here they're fed
exactly, cut short
of the smug digestive stupors
across which they drag their swag-
ridden bellies to a sleep

that smells like vomit,
acrid, carrion-soaked, stale.
They sleep off as much as they can.
The Cincinnati lions pace as clocks pace.
They measure themselves again
and again, and they fit.

# A Walk with John Logan, 1973

Roads lined by dirtied curds of snow,
I remember that. The sky over the Finger
Lakes was marled and low. I'd made pâté
for the after-reading party the night before
and my dog, that genial cadge, had slurped
a good half-pound of it, and ever since
had farted like a pan of popcorn in full
fusillade. Even in trudge, John was a scholar:
he spun out intermittently a short-
breathed paragraph on flatulence in the Greek
Anthology with, like a maraschino cherry
in a drink, an apt allusion to "Three Essays
on Infant Sexuality." I remember being young
and stupid, though time of course applied
its usual and savage remedies. John, who
waddled wisely along Krums Corners Rd.
with me, is dead, ditto the dog, and I'm
the age now he was then. I walk a little
like a duck myself, arthritic hip and all,
and just a month ago a basketball opponent
less than half my age told me, "Nice shot,
sir." I was short of breath and watery
of legs, playing a bland-faced oaf
such as I'd been myself and proud of it.
The voice I heard in my head was John's,
reedy and pinched like a bad clarinetist's,
the way George Lewis's tone or Pee Wee
Russell's tone, to name two sentimental
geniuses, was watery and flat. "They got
it wrong, the rhetoricians," he was saying.

# Clearwater Beach, Florida, 1950

Each dockpost comes with a pelican
who seems to my eight-year-old eye
to be a very distinguished bat. And then
one languidly unrumples itself and flies
off like a purposeful overcoat.

Signs on the causeway warn not to eat
the oleander leaves. A new place means
new poisons. And the palmetto grass,
and the topknotted bromeliads, and
the jellyfish like clouds of clear brains

trailing rain. . . . The scenery is in another
language, and I'm still besotted by
my own, half books and half Ohio.
A children's work is never done, so
I'm up early, stubbing my whole foot

on the sprinkler caps in the rosetted
grass. Is it too early to cry? Do I talk
too much? What does it mean to be full
of yourself, or on vacation?
There's something from church — a living

coal on the tongue — I remember. What's
a dead coal? It won't be breakfast
until the grown-ups break their blur and crust
of sleep and come downstairs, and al-
ready, once again, I'm given to language.

Though how could they have saved me?
I'm staunch in the light-blanched yard
and they're in sleep, through which their last
dreams of the morning drain,
and I'm in the small fort of my sunburnt body.

# Jilted

How quickly the landscape fills
with figures, with code, with the palpable
unspoken, where once trees,
for example, bore in each leaf
only a little slow factory
making work for itself tomorrow,
one day ahead of itself like trust.
Bent to themselves like that,
how could they serve to show
if you will come or not, or be late
merely, or disappear?
                     Now that trees
stand for something I can't
understand, and so must be figures
for articulate loss, they seem
as tragic as we are, emblems
rather than habits. If again this time
you don't come, perhaps it will be
because you are already
allegorical, and I will turn here
like a weathervane, a rooster
soldered to his useless work.

# A Happy Childhood
*(1984)*

# Good

I'd seen wallpaper — I had buckaroos all over my
bedroom — but my friend the only child had ceiling paper;
in the dark he had a flat sky, if stars make

a sky. Six feet above his bed, where the soul hovers
when the body's in doubt, he had a phosphorous
future, a lifetime of good marks for being alone.

*He's an only child, you know,* my parents would say.

OK, but I slept with no lid, like a shoe left out-
doors or an imaginary friend, with no sky to hold
him down nor light by which to watch him drift away.

Listen, my little mongoose, I know
the difference between this and love,
for I've had love, and had it taken away.

This feeling-sorry-for-ourselves-but-outward
is one of desire's shiftier shapes:
see how the deep of night is crept upon our love-

making, and how we believe what we disbelieve,
and find in our hopeful arms what we'd thought
to have thrown away, my stolen good,

the map by which we'll part, and love others.

Romantic, you could call him,

since he walks the balance beam
of his obsession like a triumphant
drunk passing a police test;

though, like a man in love
with a woman fools would find plain,
he doesn't turn aside for beauty;

he's a classicist, and studies
nightly a book so persistently good
he can't exhaust it, nor can it him.


Most of the time nothing happens here, we're fond
of saying. I love those stories and poems

an editor for *Scrotum* or *Terrorist Quarterly*
would describe that way, and besides,
every time in all my life I've said or heard

the phrase it's been a good lie, meaning
at least that crime and melodrama rates

are low enough that we can see, if we want,
the huge slow wheel of daily life, love and boredom,
turning deep in the ship-eating waters.

"The whole city of London uses the words *rich*
and *good* as equivalent terms," wrote Wesley
(1788), who failed to include in his whole city
the "honest poor," condemned by such a name
to improve their diet at the cost of honor.

"My good man" means "good for his debts,"
and not for nothing. What better faith
is there for the future than the braid of debt
we make, all of us? The day of reckoning
had better take its time: we're good for it.


I shouldn't pick on myself, but I do:
pimples and scabs and wens, warts, pustules,
the duff of the body sifting out, the dust

and sawdust of the spirit, blotches and slurs

and liver spots, the scar from the dogbite,
the plum-colored birthmark. . . . All this scuff
and tarnish and waste, these shavings

and leavings. . . . Deep in my body the future
is intact, in smolder, in the very bone,
and I dig for it like a dog, good dog.

After a week of sullen heat, the drenched air
bunched as if it needed to sneeze but couldn't,
the sky gives up its grip on itself and—good—

rain swabs the thick air sweet. The body's dirty
windows are flung open, and the spirit squints

out frankly. A kind of wink runs through
the whole failing body, and the spirit begins,

under its breath at first, talking to itself.
Mumbles, snickers, declamations, and next
it's singing loudly into the glistening streets.


Hi Mom, as athletes say on TV,
and here's a grateful hello to my mild

and courageous father. While I'm at it
I'd like to thank my teachers (though

not some—they know who they are) and
my friends, who by loving me freed

my poems from seeking love. Instead
they go their own strange ways

to peculiar moments like this one, when
the heart's good manners are their guide.

# Sympathetic

In *Throne of Blood,* when they come to kill
Macbeth, the screen goes white. No sound.
It could be that the film has broken,
so some of us look back at the booth,

but it's fog on the screen, and from it,
first in one corner and then in another,
sprigs bristle. The killers close in further —
we're already fogged in by the story —

using pine boughs for camouflage,
and Birnam Forest comes to Dunsinane.
Even in Japanese, tragedy works:
he seems to extrude the arrows

that kill him — he's like a pincushion —,
as if we grew our failures and topples,
as if there were no larger force than will,
as if his life seemed strange to us

until he gave it up, half-king, half-
porcupine. We understand. We too were fooled
by the fog and the pines, and didn't
recognize ourselves, until too late, as killers.

# Whiplash

That month he was broke,
so when the brakes to his car
went sloshy, he let them go.
Next month his mother came
to visit, and out they went
to gawk, to shop, to have something
to do while they talked besides
sitting down like a seminar
to talk. One day soon he'd fix
the brakes, or — as he joked
after nearly bashing a cab
and skidding widdershins
through the intersection
of Viewcrest and Edgecliff —
they'd fix him, one of these
oncoming days. We like
to explain our lives to ourselves,
so many of our fictions
are about causality — chess
problems (where the *?!* after
White's 16th move marks
the beginning of disaster),
insurance policies, box scores,
psychotherapy ("Were your
needs being met in this
relationship?"), readers' guides
to pity and terror —, and about
the possibility that because
aging is relentless, logic too
runs straight and one way only.

By this hope to know how
our disasters almost shatter us,
it would make sense to say
the accident he drove into
the day after his mother left
began the month he was broke.
Though why was he broke?
Because of decisions he'd made
the month before to balance
decisions the month before that,
and so on all the way back
to birth and beyond, for his
mother and father brought
to his life the luck of theirs.

And so when his car one slick day
oversped its dwindling ability
to stop itself and smacked two
parked cars and lightly kissed
another, like a satisfying
billiards shot, and all this action
(so slow in compression and
preparation) exploded so quickly,
it seemed not that his whole life
swam or skidded before him,
but that his whole life was behind
him, like a physical force,
the way a dinosaur's body
was behind its brain and the news
surged up and down its vast
and clumsy spine like an early
version of the blues; indeed,
indeed, what might he do
but sing, as if to remind himself
by the power of anthem that the body's
disparate and selfish provinces
are connected. And that's how

the police found him, full-throated,
dried blood on his white suit
as if he'd been caught in a rust-
storm, song running back and forth
along his hurt body like the action
of a wave, which is not water,
strictly speaking, but a force
that water welcomes and displays.

# Bad

Dew, sweat, grass-prickle, tantrums,

lemonade. One minute summer is all balm
and the next it's boredom and fury,

the library closed, the back yard blandly

familiar. The horizonless summer
recedes with a whoosh on all sides

like air being sucked out of a house

by a tornado, and there in the dead
center stands a child with a crumpling

face, whom somebody soon will call bad.


Beloved of mothers, too good in school and manners
to be true, can this unctuous wimp be real?

He'd be less dangerous if he had no good
at all in him, this level teaspoonful of virtue,

this festoon of fellowship, most likely
to succeed by filling in the blanks and hollows

like a fog or flood. Every morning he counts
his blessings backwards: he's not a crook,

not a recent thief, hates only the despised, and
(here it comes up his throat like a flag) he's not bad.

To pay a bad debt with bad coin, to breathe
bad air between bites (bad bites, an ortho-
dontist would say) of bad food, or worse,
food gone bad. . . .

             By such a token *bad*
means discreditable, that hope is a bad lien
on belief, as if there were no evil but mis-
judgment, bad budgeting,

                    or in the case
of those teeth, bad genes. But let's say it:
evil exists, because choice does, and because
luck does and the rage that is luck's wake.

Here's bad luck for you: on your way to buy
shoelaces you're struck by a would-be suicide
as you pass beneath the Smith Tower. He's saved
and you're maimed, and long after he's released
he comes to visit you in the hospital and you'd

rip his lungs out of his trunk with your poor bare
hands if they'd obey you anymore, though as luck
would have it, they won't. Or, after the operation
cleared out every one of his cancer cells, a new crop
of them blooms along the line of the incision.

All the wrapping paper stuffed into the fireplace
Christmas morning, and all the white and brown
bags, the wax and butcher's paper, the shimmers

and crinkles of spent foil, plastic wrap in shrivels,
the envelopes ripped open 2,500 miles away.

And the letters unfolded which are neither true
nor false, bad nor better, but all that the hurt heart

would cook or eat, or give and take. The ghosts
that swirl and stall and dive in the wind
like daunted kites. That we are all old haunts.


The granular fog gives each streetlight
an aura of bright haze, like a rumor:
it blobs as far as it can from its impulse.

The way gossip is truest about who says it,
the world we see is about the way we see;

if this is truth, it's easier than we thought.
What's bad about such truth is needing
to have it, as if it were money or love,

each of which clings to those on whom
enough has long ago, luckily, been spent.

The year I had my impacted wisdom teeth
cracked and tweezered out, I took codeine

for pain and beyond, until a day I could feel
my body faking pain; for which I rewarded it
with codeine. In this exchange the bad

marriage of mind and body was writ large,
and that a good one is work which is work's pay,

and that blame is not an explanation of pain
but a prolonging of pain, and that marriage
isn't a sacrament, although memory is.


When Williams called the tufty, stubbled
ground around the contagious hospital

"the new world," did he mean monumental
Europe was diseased and America needs,
like a fire set against a fire, a home-

made virus? I think so. These may be
the dead, the sick, those gone into rage

and madness, gone bad, but they're our dead
and our sick, and we will slake their lips
with our very hearts if we must, and we must.

# The Psychopathology of Everyday Life

Just as we were amazed to learn
that the skin itself is an organ—
I'd thought it a flexible sack,
always exact—we're stunned
to think the skimpiest mental
event, even forgetting, has meaning.
If one thinks of the sky as scenery,
like photographs of food, one stills it
with that wish and appetite,
but the placid expanse that results
is an illusion. The air is restless
everywhere inside our atmosphere
but the higher and thinner it gets
the less it has to push around
(how else do we see air?) but itself.
It seems that the mind, too,
is like that sky, not shiftless;
and come to think of it, the body
is no slouch at constant commerce,
bicker and haggle, provide and deny.
When we tire of work we should think
how the mind and body relentlessly
work for our living, though since
their labors end in death we greet
their ceaseless fealty with mixed emotions.
Of course the mind must pay attention
to itself, vast sky in the small skull.
In this we like to think we are alone:
evolutionary pride: it's lonely
at the top, self-consciousness. We forget
that the trout isn't beautiful and stupid

but a system of urges that works
even when the trout's small brain is somewhere
else, watching its shadow on the streambed,
maybe, daydreaming of food.
Even when we think we're not,
we're paying attention to everything;
this may be the origin of prayer
(and if we listen to ourselves,
how much in our prayers is well-dressed
complaint, how much we are loneliest Sundays
though whatever we do, say, or forget
is prayer and daily bread):
*Doesn't everything mean something?*
*O God who composed this dense*
*text, our only beloved planet*
—at this point the supplicants look upward—
*why have You larded it against our hope*
*with allusions to itself, and how*
*can it bear the weight of such*
*self-reference and such self-ignorance?*

# Loyal

They gave him an overdose
of anesthetic, and its fog
shut down his heart in seconds.
I tried to hold him, but he was
somewhere else. For so much of love
one of the principals is missing,
it's no wonder we confuse love
with longing. Oh I was thick
with both. I wanted my dog
to live forever and while I was
working on impossibilities
I wanted to live forever, too.
I wanted company and to be alone.
I wanted to know how they trash
a stiff ninety-five-pound dog
and I paid them to do it
and not tell me. What else?
I wanted a letter of apology
delivered by decrepit hand,
by someone shattered for each time
I'd had to eat pure pain. I wanted
to weep, not "like a baby,"
in gulps and breath-stretching
howls, but steadily, like an adult,
according to the fiction
that there is work to be done,
and almost inconsolably.

# A Happy Childhood

*Babies do not want to hear about babies;*
*they like to be told of giants and castles.*
                                    —Dr. Johnson

*No one keeps a secret so well as a child.*
                                    —Victor Hugo


My mother stands at the screen door, laughing.
"Out out damn Spot," she commands our silly dog.
I wonder what this means. I rise into adult air

like a hollyhock, I'm so proud to be loved
like this. The air is tight to my nervous body.
I use new clothes and shoes the way the corn-studded

soil around here uses nitrogen, giddily.
Ohio, Ohio, Ohio. Often I sing
to myself all day like a fieldful of August

insects, just things I whisper, really,
a trance in sneakers. I'm learning
to read from my mother and soon I'll go to school.

I hate it when anyone dies or leaves and the air
goes slack around my body and I have to hug myself,
a cloud, an imaginary friend, the stream in the road-

side park. I love to be called for dinner.
Spot goes out and I go in and the lights
in the kitchen go on and the dark,

which also has a body like a cloud's,
leans lightly against the house. Tomorrow
I'll find the sweatstains it left, little grey smudges.

Here's a sky no higher than a streetlamp,
and a stack of morning papers cinched by wire.
It's 4:00 A.M. A stout dog, vaguely beagle,

minces over the dry, fresh-fallen snow;
and here's our sleep-sodden paperboy
with his pliers, his bike, his matronly dog,

his unclouding face set for paper route
like an alarm clock. Here's a memory
in the making, for this could be the morning

he doesn't come home and his parents
two hours later drive his route until
they find him asleep, propped against a streetlamp,

his papers all delivered and his dirty paper-
satchel slack, like an emptied lung,
and he blur-faced and iconic in the morning

air rinsing itself a paler and paler blue
through which a last few dandruff-flecks
of snow meander casually down.

The dog squeaks in out of the dark,
snuffling *me too me too*. And here he goes
home to memory, and to hot chocolate

on which no crinkled skin forms like infant ice,
and to the long and ordinary day,
school, two triumphs and one severe

humiliation on the playground, the past
already growing its scabs, the busride home,
dinner, and evening leading to sleep

like the slide that will spill him out, come June,
into the eye-reddening chlorine waters
of the municipal pool. Here he goes to bed.

Kiss. Kiss. Teeth. Prayers. Dark. Dark.
Here the dog lies down by his bed,
and sighs and farts. Will he always be

this skinny, chicken-bones?
He'll remember like a prayer
how his mother made breakfast for him

every morning before he trudged out
to snip the papers free. Just as
his mother will remember she felt

guilty never to wake up with him
to give him breakfast. It was Cream
of Wheat they always or never had together.

It turns out you are the story of your childhood
and you're under constant revision,
like a lonely folktale whose invisible folks

are all the selves you've been, lifelong,
shadows in fog, grey glimmers at dusk.
And each of these selves had a childhood

it traded for love and grudged to give away,
now lost irretrievably, in storage
like a set of dishes from which no food,

no Cream of Wheat, no rabbit in mustard
sauce, nor even a single raspberry,
can be eaten until the afterlife,

which is only childhood in its last
disguise, all radiance or all humiliation,
and so it is forfeit a final time.

In fact it was awful, you think, or why
should the piecework of grief be endless?
Only because death is, and likewise loss,

which is not awful, but only breathtaking.
There's no truth about your childhood,
though there's a story, yours to tend,

like a fire or garden. Make it a good one,
since you'll have to live it out, and all
its revisions, so long as you all shall live,

for they shall be gathered to your deathbed,
and they'll have known to what you and they
would come, and this one time they'll weep for you.


The map in the shopping center has an X
signed "you are here." A dream is like that.
In a dream you are never eighty, though

you may risk death by other means:
you're on a ledge and memory calls you
to jump, but a deft cop talks you in

to a small, bright room, and snickers.
And in a dream, you're everyone somewhat,
but not wholly. I think I know how that

works: for twenty-one years I had a father
and then I became a father, replacing him
but not really. Soon my sons will be fathers.

Surely, that's what middle-aged means,
being father and son to sons and father.
That a male has only one mother is another

story, told wherever men weep wholly.
Though nobody's replaced. In one dream
I'm leading a rope of children to safety,

through a snowy farm. The farmer comes out
and I have to throw snowballs well to him
so we may pass. Even dreaming, I know

he's my father, at ease in his catcher's
squat, and that the dream has revived
to us both an old unspoken fantasy:

we're a battery. I'm young, I'm brash,
I don't know how to pitch but I can
throw a lamb chop past a wolf. And he

can handle pitchers and control a game.
I look to him for a sign. I'd nod
for anything. The damn thing is hard to grip

without seams, and I don't rely only
on my live, young arm, but throw by all
the body I can get behind it, and it fluffs

toward him no faster than the snow
in the dream drifts down. Nothing
takes forever, but I know what the phrase

means. The children grow more cold
and hungry and cruel to each other
the longer the ball's in the air, and it begins

to melt. By the time it gets to him we'll be
our waking ages, and each of us is himself
alone, and we all join hands and go.


Toward dawn, rain explodes on the tin roof
like popcorn. The pale light is streaked by grey
and that green you see just under the surface

of water, a shimmer more than a color.
Time to dive back into sleep, as if into
happiness, that neglected discipline. . . .

In those sixth-grade book reports
you had to say if the book was optimistic
or not, and everyone looked at you

the same way: how would he turn out?
He rolls in his sleep like an otter.
Uncle Ed has a neck so fat it's funny,

and on the way to work he pries the cap
off a Pepsi. Damn rain didn't cool one weary
thing for long; it's gonna be a cooker.

The boy sleeps with a thin chain of sweat
on his upper lip, as if waking itself,
becoming explicit, were hard work.

Who knows if he's happy or not?
A child is all the tools a child has,
growing up, who makes what he can.

# Civilization and Its Discontents

*Integration in, or adaptation to, a human community*
*appears as a scarcely avoidable condition which must be*
*fulfilled before [our] aim of happiness can be achieved.*
*If it could be done without that condition, it would*
*perhaps be preferable.*

*—Freud*


How much of the great poetry
of solitude in the woods is one
long cadenza on the sadness

of civilization, and how much
thought on beaches, between drowsing
and sleep, along the borders,

between one place and another,
as if such poise were home to us?
On the far side of these woods, stew,

gelatinous from cracked lamb shanks,
is being ladled into bowls, and
a family scuffs its chairs close

to an inherited table.
Maybe there's wine, maybe not. We don't
know because our thoughts are with

the great sad soul in the woods again.
We suppose that even now
some poignant speck of litter

borne by the river of psychic murmur
has been grafted by the brooding soul
to a beloved piece of music,

and that from the general plaint
a shape is about to be made, though
maybe not: we can't see into

the soul the way we can into
that cottage where now they're done with food
until next meal. Here's what I think:

the soul in the woods is not alone.
All he came there to leave behind
is in him, like a garrison

in a conquered city. When he goes
back to it, and goes gratefully
because it's nearly time for dinner,

he will be entering himself,
though when he faced the woods,
from the road, that's what he thought then, too.

# Familial

When the kitchen is lit by lilacs
and everyone's list is crumpled or forgot,
when love seems to work without plans

and to use, like an anthill, all its frenetic
extra energy, then we all hold,
like a mugful of cooling tea,

my grandmother's advice: *Don't ever
grow old.* But I'm disobedient
to the end, eager to have overcome

something, to be laved by this light,
to have gone to the heaven of grown-ups
even if my body cracks and sputters

and my young heart grows too thick.
I want my place in line, the way
each word in this genial chatter

has its place. That's why we call it
grammar school, where we learn to behave.
I understand why everyone wants

to go up to heaven, to rise,
like a ship through a curriculum
of locks, into the eternal light

of talk after dinner. What I don't
understand is why one would balk to die
if death were entry to such heaven.

# Right

We always talked about getting it right,
and finally, by making it smaller and smaller,
like inept diamond cutters, we did. We chiseled
love's radiant play and refraction

to a problem in tact and solved it
by an exact and mannerly contempt,

by the arrogance of severity,
by stubble, by silence, by grudge,
by mistaking sensibility for form,
by giving ourselves up to be right.


You have the right to be silent, blank
as an unminted coin, sullen or joyfully

fierce, how would we know? What's truly yours
you'll learn irremediably from prison.

You have the right to clamp your eyes shut,
not to assent nor to eat nor to use our only

toilet in your turn, but to hold your breath
and frail body like secrets, and to turn blue

and to be beautiful briefly to yourself.
And we have our rights, too, which you can guess.

There's fan belts stiffening out back for cars
they haven't made in fifteen years, but if one
of them geezer wagons wobbles in here, we got

the right fan belt for it. We got a regular
cat with a fight-crimped ear and a yawn pinker
than cotton candy in fluorescent light, and we

got the oldest rotating Shell sign on Route 17;
hell, we're a museum. You can get halfway
from here to days beyond recall, and the last

half you never had a chance at, from the start.


Too right, my son accuses me when I correct
his grammar, but then, like an anaconda
digesting a piglet and stunned by how much blood
he needs to get this one thing done, he pales,

and then he's gone, slipped totally inside
himself, someplace I can't get from here
or anywhere, and now I need to tease him out
from his torpid sulk, or to wait till he slithers

out on his own. Come to think of it, that's how
I got here, eager, willful, approximate.

Four months of his life a man spends shaving,
a third of it asleep or pacing his room in want
of the civil wilderness of sleep, like a zoo lion

surveying the domain of its metabolism,
and what slice of his life does he pass

mincing shallots, who loves cooking?
If time is money, it's inherited
wealth, a relic worn smooth and then

worn to nothing by pilgrims' kisses,
and there's no right way to keep or spend it.


Right as rain you are, rain that shrivels
the grapes and then plumps the raisins.
You were right when you felt peeled,
like a crab in molt, and right you were

when you chafed stiffly against your shell

and wanted out. You're condemned to be right,
to agonize with what's right as the future
invades you and to explain the inevitable
past as it leaves you to colonize yourself,

to be you, finally to stand up for your rights.

Gauche, sinister, but finally harmless because
flaky, somehow miswired, a southpaw

(there's no more a northpaw than there is a soft-
nosed realist: the curse and blazon of rectitude
is that even the jokes about you are dull,

and your fire is embers and cozy, grey at the edge
and pink in the middle, like a well-cooked steak),

a figure of fun, as someone outnumbered so often
is, and all because you bring me, and you're right,
my irresistible self, hand outstretched, in the mirror.


On the way to the rink one fog- and sleep-thick
morning we got the work *fuck* spat at us,

my sister fluffed for figure skating and I in pads
for hockey. The slash of casual violence in it
befuddled me, and when I asked my parents
I got a long, strained lecture on married love.

Have I remembered this right? The past is lost
to memory. Under the Zamboni's slathering tongue
the ice is opaque and thick. Family life is easy.
You just push off into heartbreak and go on your nerve.

# The Theme of the Three Caskets

*Men and women are two locked caskets,*
*each of which contains the key to the other.*
                                        —*Isak Dinesen*


One gold, one silver, one lead: who thinks
this test easy has already flunked.

Or, you have three daughters, two humming-
birds and the youngest, Cordelia, a grackle.

And here's Cinderella, the ash-princess.
Three guesses, three wishes, three strikes and

you're out. You've been practicing for this
for years, jumping rope, counting out,

learning to waltz, games and puzzles,
tests and chores. And work, in which strain

and ease fill and drain the body like air
having its way with the lungs. And now?

Your palms are mossy with sweat.
The more you think the less you understand.

It's your only life you must choose, daily.


Freud, father of psychoanalysis,
the study of self-deception and survival,
saw the wish-fulfillment in this theme:

that we can choose death and make what we can't
refuse a trophy to self-knowledge, grey,
malleable, dense with low tensile strength

and poisonous in every compound.
And that a vote for death elects love.
If death is the mother of love (Freud wrote

more, and more lovingly, on mothers
than on fathers), she is also the mother
of envy and gossip and spite, and she

loves her children equally. It isn't mom
who folds us finally in her arms,
and it is we who are elected.


✓      Is love the reward, or the test itself?

That kind of thought speeds our swift lives
along. The August air is stale in

the slack leaves, and a new moon thin
as a fingernail-paring tilts orange

and low in the rusty sky, and the city
is thick with trysts and spats,

and the banked blue fires of TV sets,
and the anger and depression that bead

on the body like an acid dew when it's hot.
Tonight it seems that love is what's

missing, the better half. But think
with your body: not to be dead is to be

sexual, vivid, tender and harsh, a riot
of mixed feelings, and able to choose.

# Masterful

They say you can't think and hit at the same time,
but they're wrong: you think with your body, and the whole

wave of impact surges patiently through you
into your wrists, into your bat, and meets the ball

as if this exact and violent tryst had been a fevered
secret for a week. The wrists "break," as the batting

coaches like to say, but what they do is give away
their power, spend themselves, and the ball benefits.

When Ted Williams took—we should say "gave"—
batting practice, he'd stand in and chant to himself

"My name is Ted Fucking Ballgame and I'm the best
fucking hitter in baseball," and he was, jubilantly

grim, lining them out pitch after pitch, crouching
and uncoiling from the sweet ferocity of excellence.

# An Elegy for Bob Marley

In an elegy for a musician,
one talks a lot about music,
which is a way to think about time
instead of death or Marley,

and isn't poetry itself about time?
But death is about death and not time.
Surely the real fuel for elegy
is anger to be mortal.

No wonder Marley sang so often
of an ever-arriving future, that verb tense
invented by religion and political rage.
*Soon come.* Readiness is all,

and not enough. From the urinous
dust and sodden torpor
of Trenchtown, from the fruitpeels
and imprecations, from cunning,

from truculence, from the luck
to be alive, however, cruelly,
Marley made a brave music —
a rebel music, he called it,

though music calls us together,
however briefly — and a fortune.
One is supposed to praise the dead
in elegies for leaving us their songs,

though they had no choice; nor could
the dead bury the dead if we could pay

them to. This is something else we can't
control, another loss, which is, as someone

said in hope of consolation,
only temporary, though the same phrase
could be used of our lives and bodies
and all that we hope survives them.

# Wrong

There's some wrong that can't be salved,
something irreversible besides aging.

This salt, like a light in the wound it rankles. . . .
It seems the wound might exist to uncover
the salt, the anger, the petulance we hoard

cell by cell, treasure the body can bury.
As J. Paul Getty knew, the meek will

inherit the earth, but not the mineral rights.
And what's our love for the future but greed,
who can't let go the unbearable past?



By itself *wrong* spreads nearly five pages
in the *OED*, and meant in its ancestral forms
*curved, bent, the rib of a ship* — neither
straight, nor true, but apt for its work.

The heart's full cargo is so immense it's not

hard to feel the weight of the word
shift, and we might as well admit it's easy
to think of the spites and treacheries
and worse the poised word had to bear

lest some poor heart break unexplained, inept.

It's wrong to sleep late and wake like a fog,
and to start each paragraph of a letter with I,

and wrong to be cruel to others, the swarms
of others damp from their mutual exhalations,

and wrong to complain more than once
if others are cruel to you, wrong to be lonely,

to come home in spirals and not to unscrew
but to whistle and twist by yourself like a seed

which the wind will know how to carry
and the wind will know when to drop.


It's too quiet out there. There's something wrong.
I smell a rat. You can't fire me, I quit, the boss
will never pay enough, it's so hot in here I think

I'll take off my job. Then I ripped off her dress, then
I hit her, I was like a wild man, except I was ashamed.

I've read about creeps in the papers, they hear voices
and don't disobey. I don't obey one, not even me,

and I'm all of my voices. Creeps, I said, and Creeps,
I sang, but I'm one. So are you. Let me buy you a beer.
I'll bet you're full of good stories. Let me buy you another.

Even in sleep, the world is smaller. In a dream
I want you to go somewhere with me, and you
won't come. When I wake there's fog at the waists

of the trees, like a sash. There are treetops
and treetrunks, and a smear where the two don't
join. It's wrong to be in this much pain. The bay
is out there somewhere. Yes. I can hear someone

singing badly over the waters. No. It's a radio
with a cracked speaker drilling through the fog,
faithfully towing a lobsterboat to its traps.


Maybe what's wrong, if *wrong* is the right word,
is that we like to think the body is defending us,
as if when some part of the world gets in you
that shouldn't, you're done for, and so

your antibodies run wild and do not stop
when the work they're designed for is done,

but they rage against the very body. What
little I know of the mind, I know it sometimes
works like that, if *works* is the right word,
and it is. Not the body, nor the mind, has a boss.

What's wrong is to live by correction, to be good
for a living—proofreader, inspector of public works—,

to go into the tunnels of error like a rat terrier
and come out and know you will be fed for it.
Sop, mash, some dark velvety food rich as bogbottom,

some archival soup with one of every nutrient,
an unbearably dense Babel of foodstuffs, what you get

for knowing wrong when you see it, for knowing
what to do next and doing it well, for eating
the food and knowing there is nothing wrong with it.


Corms and bulbs into the ground, bone meal
buried with them like a pharaoh's retainers,
and an exact scatter of bark on top for mulch. . . .

And the rank weeds winter down there, too,
as if the mulch were strewn for them, as if
diligent worms broke ground for them; and who's

to say, turning this soil, that they're wrong?
The detection of wrong and the study of error
are lonely chores; though who is wrong by himself,

and who is by himself except in error?

# Foreseeable Futures

*(1987)*

# Fellow Oddballs

The sodden sleep from which we open like umbrellas,
the way money keeps *us* in circulation, the scumbled lists
we make of what to do and what, God help us, to undo—

an oddball knows an oddball at forty or at 40,000
paces. Let's raise our dribble glasses. Here's to us,
morose at dances and giggly in committee,

and here's to us on whose ironic bodies new clothes
pucker that clung like shrink wrap to the manikins.
And here's to the threadbare charm of our self-pity.

For when the waiters, who are really actors between parts,
have crumbed for the last time our wobbly tables,
and we've patted our pockets for keys and cigarettes

enough until tomorrow, for the coat-check token
and for whatever's missing, well then, what next? God knows,
who counts us on God's shapely toes, one and one and one.

# April in the Berkshires

Dogs skulk, clouds moil and froth, humans
begin to cook — butter, a blue waver of flame,
chopped onions. A styptic rain stings grit and soot

from the noon air. Here and there, like the mess
after a party, pink smudgily tinges the bushes,
but they'll be long weeks of mud and sweaters

before a finch dips and percolates through
the backyard air like the talk of old friends.
It feels like the very middle, the exact

fulcrum of our lives. Our places wait for us
in the yard, like shadows furled in bud.
On the chill wands of the forsythia pale

yellow tatters wave. How long has Mr. Forsyth
been dead? Onto the lawn we go.
Lights, camera, action: the story of our lives.

# Photo of the Author with a Favorite Pig

Behind its snout like a huge button,
like an almost clean plate, the pig
looks candid compared to the author,

and why not? He has a way with words,
but the unspeakable pig, squat
and foursquare as a bathtub,

squints frankly. Nobody knows
the trouble it's seen, this rained-out
pork roast, this ham escaped into

its corpulent jokes, its body of work.
The author is skinny and looks serious:
what will he say next? The copious pig

has every appearance of knowing,
from his pert, coiled tail to the wispy tips
of his edible ears, but the pig isn't telling.

# The Accompanist

Don't play too much, don't play
too loud, don't play the melody.
You have to anticipate her
and to subdue yourself.
She used to give me her smoky
eye when I got boisterous,
so I learned to play on tip-
toe and to play the better half
of what I might. I don't like
to complain, though I notice
that I get around to it somehow.
We made a living and good music,
both, night after night, the blue
curlicues of smoke rubbing their
staling and wispy backs
against the ceilings, the flat
drinks and scarce taxis, the jazz life
we bitch about the way Army pals
complain about the food and then
re-up. Some people like to say
with smut in their voices how playing
the way we did at our best is partly
sexual. OK, I could tell them
a tale or two, and I've heard
the records Lester cut with Lady Day
and all that rap, and it's partly
sexual but it's mostly practice
and music. As for partly sexual,
I'll take wholly sexual any day,
but that's a duet and we're talking
accompaniment. Remember "Reckless

Blues"? Bessie Smith sings out "Daddy"
and Louis Armstrong plays back "Daddy"
as clear through his horn as if he'd
spoken it. But it's her daddy and her
story. When you play it you become
your part in it, one of her beautiful
troubles, and then, however much music
can do this, part of her consolation,
the way pain and joy eat off each other's
plates, but mostly you play to drunks,
to the night, to the way you judge
and pardon yourself, to all that goes
not unsung, but unrecorded.

# Herd of Buffalo Crossing the Missouri on Ice

If dragonflies can mate atop the surface tension
of water, surely these tons of bison can mince
across the river, their fur peeling in strips like old

wallpaper, their huge eyes adjusting to how far
they can see when there's no big or little bluestem,
no Indian grass nor prairie cord grass to plod through.

Maybe because it's bright in the blown snow
and swirling grit, their vast heads are lowered
to the gray ice: nothing to eat, little to smell.

They have their own currents. You could watch a herd
of running pronghorn swerve like a river rounding
a meander and see better what I mean. But

bison are a deeper, deliberate water, and there will
never be enough water for any West but the one
into which we watch these bison carefully disappear.

# Caddies' Day, the Country Club,
# a Small Town in Ohio

On Mondays even the rich work,
we'd joke around the caddy shack,
though our idea of the rich
was Buick dealers we resented
for their unappeasable daughters.
Mondays the club was closed
except to us, who toiled around
its easy eighteen holes: three hills,
six traps. The water hazard was the pool.
We'd play as slowly as we could,
as if to stretch a day of rest
weeklong. That's any Monday but
the one Bruce Ransome came up
from the bottom of the pool
like a negative rising in a tank,
his body clear, dead, abstract.
Our ignorance lay all around us
like a landscape. So this
is the surface of earth, this loam
so fecund it's almost money,
the top half dredged from Canada
by kindly glaciers, the bottom
ours by blind luck, nature's version
of justice. So this is the first death.
And there I was, green as the sick
and dying elephant in the Babar
book I thought I had outgrown.
That elephant was so wrinkled
he might have drowned over and over,
like a character in a story

whom the author had made unlucky.
The lucky stand in a green stupor
like a beautiful forest. And
their gossip is about how the lucky
link arms, and the living, how the surface
bears us up from Monday to Monday
like a story about persistence,
so that the long work of memory
goes on, its boredom and its courage
and its theology of luck, which
is finally a contest that luck wins.
Do you want my premature stroke?
Do I want your retarded child?
Do you want Bruce Ransome green
in your dowsing arms you can't link
anymore with mine, they're so full
of death-rinsed Bruce, or do you want
to lay him down forever,
one long Monday to the next
and to the next one after that,
and let the long week adhere
to your fingers like grime, like matter's
fingerprints, like manual labor,
like an entire life's work?

# Dog Life

Scuffed snout, infected ear, ticks like interest
on a loan. Butt of jokes that would, forgive me,
raise hair on a bald dog. Like the one about the baby

so ugly that to get a dog to play with it,
they had to tie a pork chop around the baby's neck.
Or, get this, when you're not working like a dog,

you're dogging it. Yet those staunch workers,
human feet, are casually called dogs, and they're
like miners or men who work in submarines,

hard men who call each other sons of bitches
when they're mad. No wonder it's not loyalty
to dogs that dogs are famous for, since it's men

who've made dogs famous. And don't we under-
stand about having masters, and having food?
Masters are almost good enough for us.

# Recovery Room

How bright it would be, I'd been warned.
To my left an old woman keened steadily,
*Help me, help me,* and steadily a nurse delivered
false and stark balm to her crumpled ear:
*You'll be all right.* Freshly filleted, we lay

drug-docile on our rolling trays, each boat
becalmed in its slip. I was numb waist-down
to wherever I left off, somewhere between my waist
and Budapest, for I was pointed feet-first east.
I had the responsibility of legs, like tubes

of wet sand, but no sensation from them.
Anyone proud of his brain should try to drag
his body with it before bragging. I had to wait
for my legs and bowels and groin to burn
not with their usual restlessness but

back toward it from anesthetic null. I felt—
if *feel* is the right verb here—like a diver
serving time against the bends. And O
there were eight of us parked parallel
as piano keys against the west wall of that

light-shrill room, and by noon we were seven,
though it took me until I got to the surface
to miss her. Especially if half of me's been trans-
planted by Dr. Flowers, the anesthesiologist,
I'm divided, forgetful. I hated having an equator,

below which my numb bowels stalled and my bladder
dully brimmed. A terrible remedy for these
drug-triggered truancies was "introduced,"
as the night nurse nicely put it, and all
the amber night I seeped into a plastic pouch,

and by dawn, so eager was I to escape, and ever
the good student, I coaxed my bowels to turn
a paltry dowel. Here was proof for all of us:
my legs were mine to flee on once again.
Even a poet can't tell you how death enters

an ear, but an old woman whose grating voice
I hated and whose pain I feared died next to me
while I waited like a lizard for the first fizzles
of sensation from my lower, absent, better half:
and like a truculent champagne,

the bottom of my body loosed a few
petulant bubbles, then a few more,
and then. . . . You know the rest.
Soon they let me go home and I did.
*Welcome back,* somebody said. Back? Back?

# Black Box

Because the cockpit, like the snowy village in a paperweight,
parodies the undomed world outside, and because
even a randomly composed society like Air Florida

flight #7 needs minutes for its meeting, the tape
in the black box slithers and loops with its slow,
urinary hiss like the air-filtering system in a fall-

out shelter. What's normally on the tape? Office life
at 39,000 feet, radio sputter and blab, language
on automatic pilot. Suppose the flight should fail.

Cosseted against impact and armored against fire,
the black box records not time but history. Bad choice.
The most frequent last word on the black box

tape is "Mother." Will this change if we get
more female pilots? Who knows? But here's
the best exchange: "We're going down." "I know."

# Vasectomy

After the vas deferens is cut, the constantly
manufactured sperm cells die into the bloodstream
and the constant body produces antibodies

to kill them. Dozens of feet of coiled wiring
need to be teased out and snipped at the right spot,
and then, local anesthetic winding down, the doc

has to stuff it all back in like a flustered motorist
struggling to refold a road map. But never mind,
you'll fire blanks forever after. At first you may feel

peeled and solitary without your gang of unborn
children, so like the imaginary friends of childhood
and also like those alternate futures you'll never

live out and never relinquish because they're company,
and who'd blame you preferring company to love?
Most of the other animals live in groups we've named

so lavishly we must love them. Lions: a pride.
Foxes: a skulk. Larks: an exaltation. And geese:
a skein in the sky and a gaggle on the ground.

Venereal nouns, they're called, for the power Venus
had to provoke allegiances. But the future comes
by subtraction. The list dwindles of people

you'd rather be than you. Nobody in a dream
is dead, so when you wake at 5:00 A.M. to scuffle
across the hall and pee, to lower your umber line

and reel it back in dry, and then to lie back down
and bob like a moored boat two hours more,
you think how if you brought them all — the dead,

the living, the unborn — promiscuously on stage
as if for bows, what a pageant they'd make!
They would. They do. But by then you're back to sleep.

# Blues If You Want

*(1989)*

# Nabokov's Blues

The wallful of quoted passages from his work,
with the requisite specimens pinned next
to their literary cameo appearances, was too good

a temptation to resist, and if the curator couldn't,
why should we? The prose dipped and shimmered
and the "flies," as I heard a buff call them, stood

at lurid attention on their pins. If you love to read
and look, you could be happy a month in that small
room. One of the Nabokov photos I'd never seen:

he's writing (left-handed! why did I never trouble
to find out?) at his stand-up desk in the hotel
apartment in Montreux. The picture's mostly

of his back and the small wedge of face that shows
brims with indifference to anything not on the page.
The window's shut. A tiny lamp trails a veil of light

over the page, too far away for us to read.
We also liked the chest of specimen drawers
labeled, as if for apprentice Freudians,

"Genitalia," wherein languished in phials
the thousands he examined for his monograph
on the Lycaenidae, the silver-studded Blues.

And there in the center of the room a carillon
of Blues rang mutely out. There must have been
three hundred of them. Amanda's Blue was there,

and the Chalk Hill Blue, the Karner Blue
(*Lycaeides melissa samuelis* Nabokov),
a Violet-Tinged Copper, the Mourning Cloak,

an Echo Azure, the White-Lined Green Hairstreak,
the Cretan Argus (known only from Mt. Ida:
in the series Nabokov did on this beauty

he noted for each specimen the altitude at which
it had been taken), and as the ads and lovers say,
"and much, much more." The stilled belle of the tower

was a *Lycaeides melissa melissa*. No doubt
it's an accident Melissa rhymes, sort of, with Lolita.
The scant hour we could lavish on the Blues

flew by, and we improvised a path through cars
and slush and boot-high berms of mud-blurred snow
to wherever we went next. I must have been mute,

or whatever I said won from silence nothing
it mourned to lose. I was back in that small
room, vast by love of each flickering detail,

each genital dusting to nothing, the turn,
like a worm's or caterpillar's, of each phrase.
I stood up to my ankles in sludge pooled

over a stopped sewer grate and thought —
wouldn't you know it — about love and art:
you can be ruined ("rurnt," as we said in south-

western Ohio) by a book or improved by
a butterfly. You can dodder in the slop,
septic with a rage not for order but for the love

the senses bear for what they do, for the detail
that's never annexed, like a reluctant crumb
to a vacuum cleaner, to a coherence.

You can be bead after bead on perception's rosary.
This is the sweet ache that hurts most, the way
desire burns bluely at its phosphorescent core:

just as you're having what you wanted most,
you want it more and more until that's more
than you, or it, or both of you, can bear.

# 39,000 Feet

The cap'n never drawls, *We're seven miles*
*or so above the earth and weigh more than*
*the town I grew up in.* He says, *We've reached*
*our cruising altitude.* And how we labored
to get there. We held our armrests down lest
they careen around the cabin and terrify
less experienced fliers, an acrid dew formed
on our palms, and none of us in coach
thought the word "steerage." There are certain
things the legal department has decreed
the cap'n must not say to an open microphone —
e.g., *Uh-oh* — for we have paid for tickets
and that means contract law, and these are
corporate lawyers, not the sorts who buy ad space
on matchbooks. (Spinal Injury? Slither on in
to Tort, Writ and Blackmail for a free
consultation. *Hablamos español.*) Of course
if they'd done better at law school they wouldn't
work for an airline, they'd be free lances,
though "free" seems a strange word just there
indeed. Once in a hotel lobby in St. Louis
I overheard a celebrity lawyer spit into
a pay phone that he was sick and tired of all
the little people, and if cars look like ants
from a mile up imagine what we look like now —
a needle — if he could see us through the hotel
roof; his rage; the towering curds and paling wisps
of clouds; the blue, sourceless, amniotic light
in which the world, hidden by clouds, seems
from 39,000 feet to float. Drinks and then food
rumbled down the aisle. The cap'n came back

on the horn: *How do you like the flight so far?*
*And lemme ask you all about that squall of baby*
*protest we rose through to level off. How*
*did you feel about it, and can you blame*
*the little imps?* We couldn't. We were starting
our descent. Rich as we were in misgiving
when we took off, we liked the chill and lull
of 39,000 feet, for there we felt, I'm not sure
how to say this, somehow American. The law
seemed still a beautiful abstraction, and the land
we sped so far above was like the land we grew
up on, before the malls and apartment
complexes were named for what had been destroyed
to build them: Fair Meadows Mall, Tall Oaks
Townhouses. Trapped in the same experiment,
as ever, we turned to each other
our desperate American friendliness,
now our most spurned export, and rode
down, through tufts and tatters of clouds
and through *mild chop,* into Detroit, where
cap'n bade us good-bye and then the first-
class passengers *deplaned,* and then the rest
of us, some with imps and some without.

# Mood Indigo

From the porch; from the hayrick where her prickled
brothers hid and chortled and slurped into their young pink
lungs the ash-blond dusty air that lay above the bales

like low clouds; and from the squeak and suck
of the well-pump and from the glove of rust it implied
on her hand; from the dress parade of clothes

in her mothproofed closet; from her tiny Philco
with its cracked speaker and Sunday litany
(*Nick Carter, The Shadow, The Green Hornet, Sky King*);

from the loosening bud of her body; from hunger,
as they say, and from reading; from the finger
she used to dial her own number; from the dark

loam of the harrowed fields and from the very sky;
it came from everywhere. Which is to say it was
always there, and that it came from nowhere.

It evaporated with the dew, and at dusk when dark
spread in the sky like water in a blotter, it spread, too,
but it came back and curdled with milk and stung

with nettles. It was in the bleat of the lamb, the way
a clapper is in a bell, and in the raucous, scratchy
gossip of the crows. It walked with her to school and lay

with her to sleep and at last she was well pleased.
If she were to sew, she would prick her finger with it.
If she were to bake, it would linger in the kitchen

like an odor snarled in the deepest folds of childhood.
It became her dead pet, her lost love, the baby sister
blue and dead at birth, the chill headwaters of the river

that purled and meandered and ran and ran until
it issued into her, as into a sea, and then she was its
and it was wholly hers. She kept to her room, as we

learned to say, but now and then she'd come down
and pass through the kitchen, and the screen door
would close behind her with no more sound than

an envelope being sealed, and she'd walk for hours
in the fields like a lithe blue rain, and end up
in the barn, and one of us would go and bring her in.

# Housecooling

Those ashes shimmering dully in the fireplace,
like tarnished fish scales? I swept them out.
Those tiny tumbleweeds of dust that stalled
against a penny or a paperclip under the bed?
I lay along the grain of the floorboards
and stared each pill into the vacuum's mouth.
I loved that house and I was moving out.

*What do you want to do when you grow up?*
they asked, and I never said, *I want to haunt
a house.* But I grew pale. The way the cops "lift"
fingerprints, that's how I touched the house.
The way one of my sons would stand in front
of me and say, *I'm outta here,* and he would mean
it, his crisp, heart-creasing husk delivering

a kind of telegram from wherever the rest of him
had gone — that's how I laved and scoured
and patrolled the house, and how I made my small
withdrawals and made my wan way outta there.
And then I was gone. I took what I could.
Each smudge I left, each slur, each whorl, I left
for love, but love of what I cannot say.

# Homer's Seeing-Eye Dog

Most of the time he wrote, a sort of sleep
with a purpose, so far as I could tell.
How he got from the dark of sleep
to the dark of waking up I'll never know;
the lax sprawl sleep allowed him
began to set from the edges in,
like a custard, and then he was awake —
me too, of course, wriggling my ears
while he unlocked his bladder and stream
of dopey wake-up jokes. The one
about the wine-dark pee I hated instantly.
I stood at the ready, like a god
in an epic, but there was never much
to do. Oh, now and then I'd make a sure
intervention, save a life, whatever.
But my exploits don't interest you,
and of his life all I can say is that
when he'd poured out his work
the best of it was gone and then he died.
He was a great man and I loved him.
Not a whimper about his sex life —
how I detest your prurience —
but here's a farewell literary tip:
I myself am the model for Penelope.
Don't snicker, you hairless moron,
I know so well what "faithful" means
there's not even a word for it in Dog.
I just embody it. I think you bipeds
have a catch phrase for it: "To thine own self

be true . . . ," though like a blind man's shadow,
the second half is only there for those who know
it's missing. Merely a dog, I'll tell you
what it is: ". . . as if you had a choice."

# The Blues

What did I think, a storm clutching a clarinet
and boarding a downtown bus, headed for lessons?
I had pieces to learn by heart, but at twelve

you think the heart and memory are different.
" 'It's a poor sort of memory that only works
backwards,' the Queen remarked." *Alice in Wonderland.*

Although I knew the way music can fill a room,
even with loneliness, which is of course a kind
of company. I could swelter through an August

afternoon — torpor rising from the river — and listen
to J. J. Johnson and Stan Getz braid variations
on "My Funny Valentine," and feel there in the room

with me the force and weight of what I couldn't
say. What's an emotion anyhow?
Lassitude and sweat lay all around me

like a stubble field, it was so hot and listless,
but I was quick and furtive like a fox
who has thirty miles a day metabolism

to burn off as ordinary business.
I had about me, after all, the bare eloquence
of the becalmed, the plain speech of the leafless

tree. I had the cunning of my body and a few
bars — they were enough — of music. Looking back,
it almost seems as though I could remember —

but this can't be; how could I bear it? —
the future toward which I'd clatter
with that boy tied like a bell around my throat,

a brave man and a coward both,
to break and break my metronomic heart
and just enough to learn to love the blues.

# Moonlight in Vermont

It's the very end of summer
and one night, probably this week, frost will sear,
like dry ice, a few leaves on trees that forayed
a few feet from the huddle of the woods, and there

they'll be, come morning, waving their red hands
like proud culprits.
One year mosquitoes clung to and trailed from
the walls and ceilings thick as tatty fabric,

and another rain lambasted us derisively
until the sogged lawns steeped like rice
in paddies. But each
year there's a dusk when the moon, like tonight's,

has risen early and every hue and tint of blue
creeps out, like an audience come to music,
to be warmed by the moon's pale fire. A car
or truck whisks

by on 125.
Somebody's hurrying home, I suppose.
Each blue is lined with a deeper blue, the way
an old magician's sleeves might be composed

of handkerchiefs. There's no illusion here.
It's beautiful to watch
and that's reason enough for blue after blue
to blossom, for each decaying swatch

to die into the next. The faster it goes
the less hurry I'm in for home or anywhere.
Like a vast grape the full
moon hangs above an empty Adirondack chair.

By now the moon itself is blue. By this
we mean that we can see in it the full freight
of our unspent love for it, for the blue night,
and for the hour, which is late.

# Smoke Gets in Your Eyes

I love the smoky libidinal murmur
of a jazz crowd, and the smoke coiling
and lithely uncoiling like a choir
of vaporous cats. I like to slouch back
with that I'll-be-here-awhile tilt
and sip a little Scotch and listen,
keeping time and remembering the changes,
and now and then light up a cigarette.

It's the reverse of music: only a small
blue slur comes out — parody and rehearsal,
both, for giving up the ghost. There's a nostril-
billowing, sulphurous blossom from the match,
a dismissive waggle of the wrist,
and the match is out. What would I look like
in that thumb-sucking, torpid, eyes-glazed
and happy instant if I could snare myself

suddenly in a mirror, unprepared by vanity
for self-regard? I'd loose a cumulus of smoke,
like a speech balloon in the comic strips,
though I'd be talking mutely to myself,
and I'd look like I love the fuss of smoking:
hands like these, I should be dealing blackjack
for a living. And doesn't habit make us
predictable to ourselves? The stubs pile up

and ashes drift against the ashtray rims
like snow against a snow fence. The boy
who held his breath till he turned blue
has caught a writhing wisp of time itself

in his long-suffering lungs. It'll take years—
he'll tap his feet to music, check his watch
(you can't fire him; he quits), shun fatty foods—
but he'll have his revenge; he's killing time.

# School Days

Once those fences kept me in. Mr. Mote
threw a dictionary at me in that room
on the corner, second floor, he and I
hypnotized by spite and everyone else
docile by default, for all we had was

fourth-grade manners: two gasped,
three tittered, Laneta hid her lovely head,
six palely watched their shoes as if they'd
brim and then flood urine, and the rest . . .
Good God, I'd forgot the rest. It's been

thirty-some years. The smart-ass afternoon
I loved them all and today all I can remember
is the name of one I loved and one I hated.
Wasn't he right to hurl at me a box
of words? By the time the dictionary spun

to rest under the radiator, its every page
was blank and the silent room was strewn
with print. I can't remember how we found
something to do, to bore up through that pall.
It would be as hard as that to remember

all their names — though, come to think of it,
I can. Isn't that how I got here,
and with you? I'm going to start at the north-
east corner of that hallucinated room
and name them one by one and row by row.

# Little Blue Nude

Outside, the crackhead who panhandles an eight-
hour day at 106th and Broadway croons
for Earl, his man, to let him in and make him well.
Soon the super's son will take his triumvirate

of dogs across the street to crap in Central Park.
Through my wall I'll hear the scrabble of their claws
and the low whirl of near-barks in their throats
as they tug their leashes down the hall and out

the door. The night a burglar forced the gate
across my kitchen window and slithered in to clean
me out, those dogs slept next door like drunken clouds.
I was in Tennessee. When I got off the plane there,

my host glanced at my tiny bag and asked, "Those
all your worldly goods?" I know you didn't ask me
what they took, but you can guess you're going to hear
the list. People tell these stories until they've worn

them out. A TV and a tape deck, two phones,
an answering machine, an alarm clock that didn't
work—these you'd expect, for they can be most
easily swept, like flecks of silt, into the swift

currents of the River Fence. The anomalies
make such lists interesting. These were mine:
two sets of sheets and pillowcases, and a bottle
of Côte Roti, 1982. Now these were clues. Also

he left my typewriter. And I knew right away
who'd robbed me. The mere pressure of my key
in the lock, before I'd even turned it, swung my door
open and my body knew he'd come in through

the kitchen but left like a guest by the front door.
Tony, my dumpster-diving friend, would bring by
things to sell: a ream of letterhead stationery
from The Children's Aid Society and two half

gallons of orange juice. Three dollars. "Whoo," he'd say.
"Ain't it a wonder what people will throw out."
So you see I was a sort of fence myself. "Being
a writer, you could probably use some paper"

was the way he'd introduced himself. The night
before I left for Tennessee he'd pasted his girlfriend
Shirley in the eye and she came by my apartment
to complain. I gave her some ice cubes nested

in a kitchen towel to hold against her bruise,
and a glass of wine. So that explains the Côte Roti.
As for the sheets, when I confronted Tony,
he yelled at me, "A dick don't have no conscience."

Speak for yourself, I thought redundantly, for I'm
the one with the typewriter and gall to speak
for others. Tony's his only clientele. "I didn't rob
your place," he yelled, "and stay away from Shirley."

The wonder is how much we manage to hang on to.
Even if a robbery's been designed to hurt,
no thief would know to take the postcard
of Renoir's *Little Blue Nude* I'd taped above my desk.

She sits, all wist and inner weather on her creamy
skin, her face bemused beneath the ginger helmet

of her hair, wholly alert to what the poets once
called reverie, perhaps, though from the relaxed

attention of her body I'd say she was listening
to beloved music. If I could choose for her,
I'd make it Ellington's 1940 recording
of "Cottontail," with Ben Webster on tenor.

If you'd been robbed, let's say, and rage ran through
you like a wind, and you balled your fists and sat
and stared at them, as though you'd forget their name,
you who are so good with words, rehearsing irate

speeches for Tony, wrapped in fury like a flower
in a bud; and also feeling impotent, a chump
with a mouthful of rant, a chump who knows
even now he'll eat the rage, the loss, the sour

tang of moral superiority to Tony,
the times he'll tell the story and list what Tony
stole . . . If you could see all those words coming
and know even now you'd eat them, every one,

you could turn to music you love, not as a mood-
altering drug nor as a consolation, but because
your emotions had overwhelmed and tired you
and made you mute and stupid, and you rued

them every one. But when Webster kicks into
his first chorus, they're back, all your emotions,
every one, and in another language, perhaps
closer to their own. "There you are," you say

to them silently, and you're vivid again, the way
we're most ourselves when we know surely
what we love, and whom. The little blue nude
has a look on her face like that. Once

when I was fussing with my tapes, Tony came by
to sell me mineral water and envelopes.
"You writing a book on jazz or what?" "No,"
I said, "I just love these." I didn't say why,

because I didn't talk that way to Tony,
and because, come to think of it, I didn't know
that day, I didn't ask myself until later,
afterthought being the writer's specialty

and curse. But that conversation explains why
he took the tapes and left the typewriter.
Writing's my scam, he thought, and music my love.
The dogs come snuffling and scrabbling back.

This time of night the building quiets down,
the hour of soliloquists. Even with walls this thin
the neighbors don't complain when I type late.
"Still working on that book?" they ask.

"What's it about?" one asked. I didn't know
that day, I didn't ask myself until later.
It's a reverie on what I love, and whom,
and how I manage to hold on to them.

# Onions

How easily happiness begins by
dicing onions. A lump of sweet butter
slithers and swirls across the floor
of the sauté pan, especially if its
errant path crosses a tiny slick
of olive oil. Then a tumble of onions.

This could mean soup or risotto
or chutney (from the Sanskrit
*chatni,* to lick). Slowly the onions
go limp and then nacreous
and then what cookbooks call clear,
though if they were eyes you could see

clearly the cataracts in them.
It's true it can make you weep
to peel them, to unfurl and to tease
from the taut ball first the brittle,
caramel-colored and decrepit
papery outside layer, the least

recent the reticent onion
wrapped around its growing body,
for there's nothing to an onion
but skin, and it's true you can go on
weeping as you go on in, through
the moist middle skins, the sweetest

and thickest, and you can go on
in to the core, to the bud-like,
acrid, fibrous skins densely

clustered there, stalky and in-
complete, and these are the most
pungent, like the nuggets of nightmare

and rage and murmury animal
comfort that infant humans secrete.
This is the best domestic perfume.
You sit down to eat with a rumor
of onions still on your twice-washed
hands and lift to your mouth a hint

of a story about loam and usual
endurance. It's there when you clean up
and rinse the wine glasses and make
a joke, and you leave the minutest
whiff of it on the light switch,
later, when you climb the stairs.

# Straight Life

There's grit in the road, and pumice,
and grease in which too many stale fish
have been fried. There are twists of breadcrust
with flourishing settlements of gray-blue
and iridescent green, and there's a wedding
band a hurt woman flung from a taxi window.
There's loneliness richer than topsoil
in Iowa, and there are swales and hollows
of boredom that go by as if trundled
by stagehands, unloved and worse,
unnoticed. Scenery, we call it, and land-
scape, when boredom is on us like a caul.
The bells of cats dead so long their names
have been forgot are bulldozed into the road,
and tendrils of rusting chrome and flecks
of car paint with ambitious names —
*British Racing Green* and *Claret.*
Cinders and tar and sweat and tax hikes
and long-term bonds. Like a village
at the base of an active volcano,
the road is built of its history.
It's we who forget, who erred and swerved
and wandered and drove back and forth
and seemed aimless as teenagers,
though one of us steered the whole time.

.

The way it happened, see, we played in Dallas,
the state fair, for some black dance. Cat with a beautiful
white suit, Palm Beach maybe, dancing his ass
off. You look up from the charts, you see that white suit

like a banner in the center of the floor. Next thing
you know there's a big circle of people moving
back, the way you throw a rock in water and it broadcasts
rings and rings, moving back. You travel
and you travel, some things you don't forget.
Two cats in the center, one of them the cat in the white
suit and suddenly the suit was soaked-through red.

·

Coleman Hawkins used to say he'd been born
on a ship, in no country at all, though I think
he said it to remind himself how torn he felt
between being American at heart and the way
Europeans treated black musicians. This life,
it's easy to feel you've been born on the road.
You know the fine coat of dust furniture grows
just standing there? We grow it traveling.
We're on the road and the road's on us.
I used to ask myself each morning where I was
but slowly learned to know — and this is how
you tell a man who's traveled some and paid
attention — by looking at the sky. A sky's
a fingerprint. All along the road the food's
the same and no two beds you hang your toes
over the end of are. That's when you've got
a bed. Some nights we just pulled the bus
off the road like a docked boat. After some towns
there'd be a scatter of spent condoms
where we'd parked, the way in a different life
you throw coins in a fountain, to come back
or not, whichever seemed the better luck.

·

I loved her earlobes and her niblet toes
and how the crook of her elbow smelled.
I loved one of her fingers most but a new
one every day. I loved how at the onset

of desire her eyes would go a little milky
the way water does just before the surface
of it shimmers when it starts to boil.
Telling how much I loved her made me talk
as well as I can play. One time she told me
what Dame Nellie Melba said: *There's only
two things I like stiff, and one of them is Jell-o.*
Then she let loose a laugh like a dropped
drawer of silverware. Here's what I said:
*I love every juice and tuft and muscle*
*of you, honey, each nub and bog and fen,*
*each prospect and each view.* That's what
I like to say I said, though where'd I learn
to talk like that? Same place I learned to play.
You know how people always ask each other
*How you feel?* You learn to look straight
at the answer without flinching, then spend
ten years to learn your instrument.
Good luck helps, too. Of course somewhere along
that line I let my sweetie slip away. Truth is,
that was by choice. But I was with her
when I learned how some things can't be fully
felt until they're said. Including this salute.


                •


You shuffle into some dingebox and there's
an audience of six, three of them sober.
The chill fire of its name in neon bathes
the windows. In the mist outside, the stoplights
are hazy and big, like lazy memories of pleasure,
and as they change in their languorous sequence,
going green and going downtown, an explanation
beckons, but of what? Too late, it's gone. No use
in staring moodily out the window.
Whatever it is, it will be back. Tires slur
on the rainy pavement outside. You've never
looked into a mirror to watch the next thing

you do, but it would identify you to yourself
faster than anything you know. You can remember it,
and in advance, with a sure and casual
rapacity. You duck your left shoulder a little
and sweep your tongue in a slight crescent
first under your top lip, then over the bottom.
You lay a thin slather on the reed and take
on a few bars of breath. Emily Dickinson
wrote of Judge Otis Phillips Lord that *Abstinence*
*from Melody was what made him die.*
Music's only secret is silence. It's time
to play, time to tell whatever you know.

# Time & Money
## (1995)

# Grief

*E detto l'ho perché doler ti debbia!*
　　　　　—Inferno, *xxiv, 151*


Snow coming in parallel to the street,
a cab spinning its tires (a rising whine
like a domestic argument, and then
the words get said that never get forgot),

slush and backed-up runoff waters at each
corner, clogged buses smelling of wet wool . . .
The acrid anger of the homeless swells
like wet rice. *This slop is where I live, bitch,*

a sogged panhandler shrieks to whom it may
concern. But none of us slows down for scorn;
there's someone's misery in all we earn.
But like a bur in a dog's coat his rage

has borrowed legs. We bring it home. It lives
like kin among the angers of the house,
and leaves the same sharp zinc taste in the mouth:
*And I have told you this to make you grieve.*

# The Wolf of Gubbio

Not the walls of the furled city,
through which he drifted like malign sleet,
nor every vigilance, could stop him.
He came and rent some poor soul
to morsels and ate him. There was no help
nearby, so Saint Francis slogged
from Assisi to tame the wolf.
Sassetta painted this meeting.
The wolf, pert and teachable as Lassie,
has laid his licentious, vow-making right paw
in the saint's hand and meets with his
ochre eye the saint's chastening gaze.
The townspeople stand like a grove
and watch. Probably one of their faces
belonged to a patron who commissioned
Sassetta, but which face? Art remembers
a few things by forgetting many.
The wolf lived on in the nearby hills
but never ate, the story goes, another
citizen. Was Sassetta the last one,
then, to see on the piazza, like dropped
firewood, most of a leg and what may be
a forearm gnawed from both ends, lurid
with scarlet blood? None in the painting
looks at this carnage and bright waste,
nor thinks of the gnarled woods
in which the pewter-colored wolf
makes his huge home, nor measures with what work
each stone was prized from the furious ground
to build each house in Gubbio
and to lay a piazza atop the town
and to raise above it a tower.

# Mingus at The Showplace

I was miserable, of course, for I was seventeen,
and so I swung into action and wrote a poem,

and it was miserable, for that was how I thought
poetry worked: you digested experience and shat

literature. It was 1960 at The Showplace, long since
defunct, on West 4th St., and I sat at the bar,

casting beer money from a thin reel of ones,
the kid in the city, big ears like a puppy.

And I knew Mingus was a genius. I knew two
other things, but as it happened they were wrong.

So I made him look at the poem.
"There's a lot of that going around," he said,

and Sweet Baby Jesus he was right. He glowered
at me but he didn't look as if he thought

bad poems were dangerous, the way some poets do.
If they were baseball executives they'd plot

to destroy sandlots everywhere so that the game
could be saved from children. Of course later

that night he fired his pianist in mid-number
and flurried him from the stand.

"We've suffered a diminuendo in personnel,"
he explained, and the band played on.

# The Bear at the Dump

Amidst the too much that we buy and throw
away and the far too much we wrap it in,
the bear found a few items of special
interest — a honeydew rind, a used tampon,
the bone from a leg of lamb. He'd rock back
lightly onto his rear paws and slash
open a plastic bag, and then his nose —
jammed almost with a surfeit of rank
and likely information, for he would pause —
and then his whole dowsing snout would
insinuate itself a little way
inside. By now he'd have hunched his weight
forward slightly, and then he'd snatch it back,
trailed by some tidbit in his teeth. He'd look
around. What a good boy am he.
The guardian of the dump was used
to this and not amused. "He'll drag that shit
every which damn way," he grumbled
who'd dozed and scraped a pit to keep that shit
where the town paid to contain it.
The others of us looked and looked. "City
folks like you don't get to see this often,"
one year-round resident accused me.
Some winter I'll bring him down to learn
to love a rat working a length of subway
track. "Nope," I replied. Just then the bear
decamped for the woods with a marl of grease
and slather in his mouth and on his snout,
picking up speed, not cute (nor had he been
cute before, slavering with greed, his weight
all sunk to his seated rump and his nose stuck

up to sift the rich and fetid air, shaped
like a huge, furry pear), but richly
fed on the slow-simmering dump, and gone
into the bug-thick woods and anecdote.

# My Father's Body

First they take it away,
for now the body belongs to the state.
Then they open it
to see what may have killed it,
and the body had arteriosclerosis
in its heart, for this was an inside job.
Now someone must identify the body
so that the state may have a name
for what it will give away,
and the funeral people come in a stark car
shaped like a coffin with a hood
and take the body away,
for now it belongs to the funeral people
and the body's family buys it back,
though it lies in a box at the crematorium
while the mourners travel and convene.
Then they bring the body to the chapel, as they call it,
of the crematorium, and the body lies in its box
while the mourners enter and sit
and stare at the box, for the box
lies on a pedestal where the altar would be
if this were a chapel.
A rectangular frame with curtains at the sides
rises from the pedestal,
so that the box seems to fill a small stage,
and the stage gives off the familiar
illusion of being a box with one wall torn away
so that we may see into it,
but it's filled with a box we can't see into.
There's music on tape and a man in a robe
speaks for a while and I speak

for a while and then there's a prayer
and then we mourners can hear the whir
of a small motor and curtains slide
across the stage. At least for today,
I think, this is the stage that all the world is,
and another motor hums on
and we mourners realize that behind
the curtains the body is being lowered,
not like Don Giovanni to the flames
but without flourish or song
or the comforts of elaborate plot,
to the basement of the crematorium,
to the mercies of the gas jets
and the balm of the conveyor belt.
The ashes will be scattered,
says a hushed man in a mute suit,
in the Garden of Remembrance,
which is out back.
And what's left of a mild, democratic man
will sift in a heap with the residue of others,
for now they all belong to time.

# Time

*I did but taste a little honey with the end of the rod
that was in mine hand, and, lo, I must die.*
— 1 Samuel 14:43

Not *sated* first, then *sad* (the two words branch,
not far apart, from the same Indo-
European root), but kindled by longing,
you amble to the window and look out.
You feel like fire's held breath just before
fire flares out from matter, but no flare comes.
And look, a blurred oval, a ghostly kiss
has formed on the window from the breath you
didn't hold. You've got time on your hands; you've
been caught red-handed with the blues and by

the worst detective in the world, yourself.
"It was blind luck, really. I knew his next
failure to move, each mope, each sullen shrug.
I knew his thoughts as if they were my own."
Cameras flash; shutters fall like tiny
guillotines. "I don't know how. Goethe said,
*If I knew myself, I'd run.*" Of course I
didn't, and that's what broke the case open.
Only one paper used the Goethe quote:
MYSTERY WOMAN HAUNTS SELF-KNOWLEDGE CASE,

the headline blared. The article gave her
name as Gerta. "About this Swiss beauty,
nothing else is known." The time had come
(but from where? hadn't it been here always?)
for me to forgo my lush indolence.
There are places things go to be forgot:
the tip of the tongue, the back of the mind,

retirement colonies like the Linger
Longer Mobile Home Park, and memory.
Perhaps I should plan how to spend my

time, but wouldn't that, like a home movie,
prove but a way to waste the same time twice?
Maybe time's just one more inexact way
to gauge loss? But we keep more than we think.
Suppose a TV signal adventures
for years in space, then hits something solid
and adventures back. You've dozed off in front
of your TV—you've been wasting some time—
and see on the screen not flickering blue
snow but the test pattern of an El

Paso station twenty-nine years defunct,
stark as a childhood taunt or remembered
genitals. What steady company you have:
you got losses like these, you'll need two trucks
next time you move. You couldn't bear to throw
them out, you said (remember?). And now what have
you got? A gorged attic like a head cold,
a basement clogged by waste. You can't "save time"
this way or any. Nor, since it can't be
owned, can it be stolen, though afternoon

adulterers add to the tryst's fevers—
the codes and lies, the sunlight sieved by blinds,
the blank sheets and the ink at brim—the pleased
guilt of having stolen time. What might they
do for time, those from whom it got stolen?
They bowl, they shop, they masturbate before
a nap (a spot of body work at O'
Nan's Auto Service), they finish their day's
work. To begin thinking about time, we might
take all the verbs we like to think we do

to time, and turn those verbs on us, and say
that time wastes us, and time saves and buys us,
that time spends us, and time marks and kills us.
We live as the direct object of verbs
we hoped we could command. Grammar school, they called
it, and we couldn't wait to graduate.
We puffed ourselves up like a cat striving
sideways to look vast, or people who like
to be right (may God thicken their tongues, or if
they write, explode their pens). Now critics write

of my "mature work" (When, the petulant boy
in me wants to know, will they publish theirs?),
and my male friends my age and I
scan the obits every day. The word
"time" now seems, often enough, the nickname
for the phrase "time left." Suppose I didn't
go from the paper to my desk. Instead
I chaperoned my tumor every
day to radiology by subway
and rancored home with it by bus. Suppose

my job was to be nauseated and bald
from chemotherapy and still to make
the plucky joke when Procter & Gamble
sent me, "Resident," a beauty about whom
nothing else was known, hair-care products.
"Luster," the prose whispered, and "sheen." My head
looked like an egg and the prose said "coupon."
I'd have ceased calling my anxious frets about
the future "thought." On Tuesday I'd wake up
and I'd say "Tuesday," my whole essay on time.

I think that's what I'd do. I'd soldier through
the fear and fell depressions. I'd call on
what those critics like nicely to call "wit,"
i.e., the whole compressed force of my rage

and love. I'd invent whatever it took
to get me through or dead, whichever came
first. And yet we must remember this:
dire time hectors us along with it, and so
we might consider thanks. Wednesday. Thursday.
Thus water licks its steady way through stone.

# President Reagan's Visit to New York, October 1984

Pomp churned through midtown like a combine,
razing a path to the Waldorf-Astoria.
At 34th and 10th a black man

drizzled a wan froth of soap and dirt
on my windshield and paused for me to pay
to get it squeegeed off. He just wanted,

he said, to make an honest living.
I gave a dollar and he gave thanks; we
knew the going rate, and so we went,

but only a few feet. The light shone red.
The Waldorf bellboys (ages 23–
59) waited, too, and men in shades

and shiny suits with walkie-talkies
along the route the limousine would take.
Our creamiest streets were cordoned off so

pomp could clot them, and the walkie-talkies
sputtered each to each. What had the black man
or I to do with this peacockery?

The light turned green. Under a soot-slurred sky
we gave each other a parting glance.
What nation you can build on that, was ours.

# Mingus at The Half Note

Two dozen bars or so into "Better Get It
in Your Soul," the band mossy with sweat,
May 1960 at The Half Note, the rain
on the black streets outside
dusted here and there by the pale pollen
of the streetlights. Blue wreaths
of smoke, the excited calm
of the hip in congregation, the long
night before us like a view and Danny
Richmond so strung out the drums
fizz and seethe. "Ho, hole, hode it,"
Mingus shouts, and the band clatters
to fraught silence. There's a twinge
in the pianist's shoulder, but this time
Mingus focuses like a nozzle
his surge of imprecations on a sleek
black man bent chattering across
a table to his lavish date:
"This is your heritage and if you
don' wanna listen, then you got
someplace else you'd better be."
The poor jerk takes a few beats
to realize he'll have to leave
while we all watch before another
note gets played. He glowers dimly
at Mingus, like throwing a rock
at a cliff, then offers his date
a disdained arm, and they leave in single
file (she's first) and don't
look back, nor at each other.
"Don't let me constrain you revelers,"

Mingus says, and then, tamed by his own rage
for now, he kick-starts the band:
"One, two, one two three four."

# Men at My Father's Funeral

The ones his age who shook my hand
on their way out sent fear along
my arm like heroin. These weren't
men mute about their feelings,
or what's a body language for?

And I, the glib one, who'd stood
with my back to my father's body
and praised the heart that attacked him?
I'd made my stab at elegy,
the flesh made word: the very spit

in my mouth was sour with ruth
and eloquence. What could be worse?
Silence, the anthem of my father's
new country. And thus this babble,
like a dial tone, from our bodies.

# The Rookery at Hawthornden

Along this path Ben Jonson rode to visit
William Drummond. What fun those two dour
poets must have made for one another.
Under a sycamore Drummond waited.
"Welcome, royal Ben."
                              "Greetings, Hawthornden."
The good fellowship of poets always
has, like death jokes on the eve of battle,
gravel in its craw.
                              Back from Bonnyrigg
I've come with a liter of the Famous
Grouse for my room. The six weeks I have here
to read, to write, to amble and to fester
with solitude, a slut for company
and bearing like a saucer of water
my intimates, my bawds, my pretty ones,
the words I wrote that didn't mutiny—
six such weeks are hard to find, and hard
to fill. Who scrawled between pastoral poems
a few rude lines to warn us? The blotched, mottled
sky above the glen, the rain, the rusty fox,
the melodious gargle of Scots talk,
the pale scumbled blue forget-me-nots—
all these can be but a reminder that
the world's a poem we'll not learn how to write.
Not portly Horace on his Sabine Farm,
that Yaddo-for-one, nor all the English
poets who admired but never sheared a sheep
nor steered a plow through soil's dun bilge and shoals
of stone.
                    Yet from the rookery the shrill
inventions rise. From the entire black bell

of each bird the rasped song clappers forth.
Verse is easy and poetry is hard.
The brash choir, like a polyphonic heart,
beats loudly in the trees and does not ask
what poetry can do, infamous for making
nothing happen. The rooks and I rejoice
not to be mute. The day burgeons with raucous
song about the joy of a song-stuffed throat.

# Note Left for Gerald Stern in an Office I Borrowed, and He Would Next, at a Summer Writers' Conference

Welcome, good heart. I hope you like — I did —
the bust of Schiller, the reproduction
of Caspar David Friedrich's painting
of Coleridge, with his walking stick, gazing
over the peaks of German thought (the Grand
Teutons?), and the many Goethe pinups.
The life of the mind is celebrated here,

so why's the place so sad? I hate the way
academic life can function as a sort
of methadone program for the depressed,
keeping the inmates steadily fatigued
and just morose enough that a day's full
measure of glum work gets done. Cowbirds
like us will have to put in our two weeks' worth

before the studied gloom begins to leak
forth from the files, the books, the post cards sent
back by colleagues from their Fulbright venues,
Tübingen, Dubrovnik, Rome, and Oslo.
Of course our own offices wait for us
and fall is coming on. To teach, Freud warned,
is one of three impossible jobs

(the others are to govern and to cure).
To teach what you know — laughter, ignorance,
curiosity, and the erotic thrall
of work as a restraint against despair —
comes as close to freedom as anyone pays

wages for. Outside the classroom such brave words
ring dully, for failures of tolerance

coat the halls as plaque clogs an artery.
Cruelty doesn't surprise a human
much, but the drenched-in-sanctimony prose
by which the cruel christen cruelty
with a better name should rot in the mouths
of the literate. The louder they quote
Dr. Johnson, the faster I count the spoons.

Well, the grunts always kvetch about the food
and the rank morals of their officers.
Who'd want to skip that part? In the office,
though, alone with the books, post cards, busts,
and sentimental clutter, we feel rage
subside and joy recede. These dusty keepsakes
block from view the very love they're meant to be

an emblem of, the love whose name is books.
Suppose we'd been kidnapped by the space
people and whisked around the galaxies,
whirred past wonders that would render Shakespeare
mute and make poor stolid Goethe whimper
like a beagle. The stellar dust, debris
agleam in the black light, the fell silence,

the arrogantly vast scale of the creation,
the speed of attack and decay each blurred,
incised impression made, the sure greed
we'd feel to describe our tour, and how we'd fail
that greed . . . And then we're back, alone
not with the past but with how fast the past
eludes us, though surely, friend, we were there.

# Cheap Seats, the Cincinnati Gardens, Professional Basketball, 1959

The less we paid, the more we climbed. Tendrils
of smoke lazed just as high and hung there, blue,
particulate, the opposite of dew.
We saw the whole court from up there. Few girls
had come, few wives, numerous boys in molt
like me. Our heroes leapt and surged and looped
and two nights out of three, like us, they'd lose.
But "like us" is wrong: we had no result
three nights out of three: so we had heroes.
And "we" is wrong, for I knew none by name
among that hazy company unless
I brought her with me. This was loneliness
with noise, unlike the kind I had at home
with no clock running down, and mirrors.

# The Rented House in Maine

At dawn, the liquid clatter of rain
pocks the bay and stutters on the roof.
Even when it's this gray, the first slant light
predicts across the rug gaunt shadows
of the generic paper birds
my landlord's pasted to the eastern wall,

all glass, to fend specific birds
from bonking themselves dull or worse
against the bright blare of false sky.
From the bay the house must look
like a grade-school homeroom gussied up
for parents' night. I like to build

a small fire first thing in the morning,
drink some coffee, drive to town,
buy the *Times*, drive back to embers
the color of canned tomato soup
(made not with water but with milk).
In this house I fell — no, hurled myself —

in love, and elsewhere, day by day,
it didn't last. Tethered to lobster traps,
buoys wobble on the bay. On the slithering
surface of the water, the rain seems
to explode — chill shrapnel, and I look
away. Embers and cool coffee. Matter,

energy, the speed of light: the universe
can be explained by an equation. Everything
that goes from one side of the equal sign

is exactly replaced from the other; i.e.,
nothing much happens at a speed so fast
we scarcely notice it, but so steadily

the math always checks out. This is thought
as I know and love it. Why did that marriage
fail? I know the reasons and count the ways.
The clouds with squalls in their cheeks,
like chaws or tongues, have broken up.
The fire is down, the coffee cold, the sun is up.

# Mingus in Diaspora

You could say, I suppose, that he ate his way out,
like the prisoner who starts a tunnel with a spoon,
or you could say he was one in whom nothing was lost,
who took it all in, or that he was big as a bus.

He would say, and he did, in one of those blurred
melismatic slaloms his sentences ran — for all
the music was in his speech: swift switches of tempo,
stop-time, double time (he could *talk* in 6/8),

"I just ruined my body." And there, Exhibit A,
it stood, that Parthenon of fat, the tenant voice
lifted, as we say, since words are a weight, and music.
Silence is lighter than air, for the air we know

rises but to the edge of the atmosphere.
You have to pick up The Bass, as Mingus called
his, with audible capitals, and think of the slow years
the wood spent as a tree, which might well have been

enough for wood, and think of the skill the bassmaker
carried without great thought of it from home
to the shop and back for decades, and know
what bassists before you have played, and know

how much of this is stored in The Bass like energy
in a spring and know how much you must coax out.
How easy it would be, instead, to pull a sword
from a stone. But what's inside the bass wants out,

the way one day you will. Religious stories are rich
in symmetry. You must release as much of this hoard
as you can, little by little, in perfect time,
as the work of the body becomes a body of work.

# Tomorrow

When the tubes in the radio had refurled
for the night their flickering orange
filamental tongues; and when the fountain
of bedtalk he could hear through the wall
to his parents' room stopped gurgling,

so that he heard the wind, like a comb
with a few teeth broken, rake the papery corn-
stubble before it rose to roll a tattoo
against the skin of his window; then the boy
knew he was on his own, except for his

dopey kitten, Asterisk, and he grew
sore afraid. While the kitten teetered across
the headboard of his bed like a high-wire
walker, placing each paw where it had fit
easily when she'd been smaller, holding

her breath (Tuna Dinner), scrabbling across
with two near-falls, he lay face down, fingers
knit across the back of his head against
her flailing claws if she should topple, but
she had not. She sat in her Egyptian

doorstop pose at the end of the headboard.
And that meant he could see her, dimly, but
he could. The dark that had gathered itself
so casually — a swatch from under
the eaves, a tatter from the dry creekbed,

a burgeoning stain in the east near dusk
like a gaggle of gossips — suddenly

was black dye, and all the world a smother
of settling cloth from which a kitten
wriggled free, and thus a sleepless boy.

# Money

*We remember the fish, which we did eat in Egypt freely: the cucumbers,*
*and the melons, and the leeks, and the garlick: But now our soul is dried*
*away: there is nothing at all, beside this manna, before our eyes.*

—*Numbers* 11:4

"Honey, I don't want to shock you,
but white people aren't white,
they're pink," a rich man's cook
told me when I was six. She was beating
egg whites for lemon meringue pie,
which the boss loved. Well then,
I thought, I'll sing for my supper,
and it worked then, though later
I got Jell-O often, and for so
little grew rancid with charm.

I rode the bike and flung the daily
paper from it. I got the grades
and brought them home. I caught
the ball and threw it back and fed
the dog while the ball was in flight,
and didn't ask, "Have I got this right?"
There were those who were good
for nothing and I set myself apart
from them. I'd make myself at home
here, like a weevil in the flour,

or like the mouse behind the stove.
The cat that killed that mouse was so
lazy and fat that it lay before
its bowl to eat and lived to be sixteen.
I remember my first raise. I smoldered
with a stupid, durable pleasure for weeks:

this stuff is powerful, like alcohol,
I thought, but it wasn't stuff, it was numbers,
nothing more than squiggles of dried ink,
though they were like new muscles

(from the Latin *musculus*, "little
mouse," for the ripple under the skin).
There were people said to be smart about
money because they had a good supply,
like those who were known to have good taste
since they shared the taste of those who said so.
I didn't want smart, though knowledge sticks
to me like dust to a dog — I'm a kind
of intellectual Velcro. Still, I do
sniff around, because that's what I wanted,

my snout to the confounded, uric ground.
"Led by the nose," even your friends will say
if you can't, or won't, describe what you want.
Or "driven," it doesn't seem to matter
which, so long as the engine isn't you.
"A simple farmboy with a smattering
of Latin, my ass," Friend B tells Friend A.
"Did you notice the shoes on that peacock?"
Friendship, too, is a species of money.
You get what you need by never knowing

what you want; you ramble like a sentence
growing ever longer and carefully
avoiding verbs, so if you imagine
the exact verb you've got a space for it,
and the fit's so tight you'd not know
there'd ever been a gap but for the ache,
which is yours always, like a phantom limb.
If you're rich enough you can be haunted
by all the dross you ever wanted,
and if you're poor enough you itch

for money all the time and scratch yourself
with anger, or, worse, hope. These thoughts
aren't dark; they're garishly well lit. Let's see
what's on TV. The news — murder and floods
and something heartwarming about a dog —
and then a commercial, but for what?
A woman in a blue silk dress eases
into a gray sedan and swirls it through turn
after turn alongside the Pacific.
She drives it right onto the beach

while the sun subsides and the ocean laces
and unlaces at her feet. She walks and pouts,
hooking her slate-colored pumps on her
left index finger. She'll ruin her new
hose and doesn't care. She purses her bruised-fruit
lips, and the sea, like a dull dog,
brings back what we throw out. What do
we want, and how much will we pay
to find out, and how much never to know?
What's wrong with money is what's wrong with love:

it spurns those who need it most for someone
already rolling in it. But only
the idea of justice is about
being just, and it's only an idea.
Money's not an abstraction; it's math
with consequences, and if it's a kind
of poetry, it's another inexact way,
like time, to measure some sorrow we can't
name. The longer you think about
either, the stupider you get,

while dinner grows tepid and stale.
The dogs have come in like a draft
to beg for scraps and nobody's
at the table. The father works on tax forms.

The mother folds laundry and hums
something old and sweetly melancholy.
The children drift glumly towards fracas.
None of these usual doldrums will lift
for long if they sit down to dinner, but
there's hunger to mollify, and the dogs.

# The Generations

I've been poor, but since I'm an American
I hated it. Bills drifted through the mail
slot of the door like snow, and desperate
people who'd hired themselves out to dun
their fellow debtors phoned during dinner
to extract shame and promises from me.
"Who called, my sweet?" my wife would wanly ask.
Her hopes were dwindling for a second dress.

I'd not carried a hod, nor laid a brick,
nor tamped tar to a roof in August,
nor squeezed my body into a freshly
gouged trench in the street to thaw a city
pipe while my co-workers clomped their feet
against the cold and yelled moral support
at me. I had a typewriter and was
that dreadful thing, a serious young

literary man. The void and I stared
at each other, and I showed my throat.
In that same throat one day I'd find my voice.
I needed time, I thought, and money, too,
but I was wrong. The voice had been there all
along. I needed work that milled me
to flour and to rage. I needed to know
not only that the boss would never pay

enough, but also that if I were boss
I wouldn't pay enough unless I grew
to be a better man than I was then.
I needed not to turn my back to my

then wife and mollify, *sotto voce*
as if I were planning a tryst,
the wretch whose dire job it was to nag me.
I needed to stand short — a tiny man,

a stick figure, as my young sons, little
Shakespeares, drew me: "the poor, bare, forked
animal." Of course they draw everyone
that way, I thought, mincing garlic
one torpid afternoon, and then I saw
that they were right. Mottled by cat dander,
perfumed by peanut butter and wet sheets,
they were powerless enough to know

the radical equality of human
souls, but too coddled to know they knew it.
They could only draw it, and they blamed
their limited techniques for the great truth
that they showed, that we're made in the image
of each other and don't know it. How hard
we'll fight to keep that ignorance they had
yet to learn, and they had me as teacher.

# Cancer Talk

Of course it's not on the X-rays: tumors
have no bones. But thanks to the MRI
we see its vile flag luffing from your spine.
To own a fact you buy many rumors:

is the blob benign, or metastatic
to the bone and fatal, or curable?
There will be tests. How good were you in school?
Cells are at work on your arithmetic.

You don't have to be a good soldier.
Lymphoma is exquisitely sensitive
to radiation, but it's not what you have.
How easy it once seemed to grow older.

Don't you hate the phrase "growth experience"?
Big as a grapefruit? Big as a golf ball?
You'll learn new idioms (how good in school
were you?) like "protocol" and "exit burns."

"You'll be a cure," a jaunty resident
predicts. What if you could be you, but rid
of the malignant garrison? How would
it feel to hear in your own dialect —

not Cancer Babble but clear Broken Heart?
Bald, queasy, chemotherapeutic beau-
ty, welcome home from Port-a-Cat and eu-
phemism. Let the healing candor start.

# A Night at the Opera

"The tenor's too fat," the beautiful young
woman complains, "and the soprano
dowdy and old." But what if Otello's
not black, if Rigoletto's hump lists,
if airy Gilda and her entourage
of flesh outweigh the cello section?

In fairy tales, the prince has a good heart,
and so as an outward and visible
sign of an inward, invisible grace,
his face is not creased, nor are his limbs gnarled.
Our tenor holds in his liver-spotted
hands the soprano's broad, burgeoning face.

Their combined age is ninety-seven; there's
spittle in both pinches of her mouth;
a vein in his temple twitches like a worm.
Their faces are a foot apart. His eyes
widen with fear as he climbs to the high
B-flat he'll have to hit and hold for five

dire seconds. And then they'll stay in their stalled
hug for as long as we applaud. Franco
Corelli once bit Birgit Nilsson's ear
in just such a command embrace because
he felt she'd upstaged him. Their costumes weigh
fifteen pounds apiece; they're poached in sweat

and smell like fermenting pigs; their voices rise
and twine not from beauty, nor from the lack
of it, but from the hope for accuracy
and passion, both. They have to hit the note
and the emotion, both, with the one poor
arrow of the voice. Beauty's for amateurs.

# Uncollected Poems
*(1982–1997)*

# Another Real Estate Deal on Oahu

He was Chinese or Japanese or *haole*;
he knew someone powerful, the neighbors
hated the idea but what could they do?
By the time they knew they'd been screwed
it was too late to protest or profit.
Everyone nods. The story's got all the right
parts: real estate, corruption and race
niftily braided, and the knowing tone
in which the losers joke about lotteries.

And the prices? *Fat! Fat! Fat!*
to quote Wallace Stevens,
who knew that *money, too,*
*is a kind of poetry,* and surely
it is, for even the battered dollar,
decried and squandered everywhere,
is tethered to the gravity
of matter and endurance
and thins at its gas-lacy tip
towards abstraction and pure vision,
just like the trees on which money
famously refuses to grow.

It refuses to grow on the banyan,
that vegetal city complete with suburban sprawl;
it refuses to grow on the sago palm,
the ti, the eucalyptus, the koa;
it's not to be found in the simmer
and rust and clatter of the rain forest,
nor high in the beachfront palmtufts,
nor in the anthology of trees

in the arboretum. Like the gods,
no matter what cultures, it's everywhere
and thus it can never be found.

I've read the classics, curious
about the gods, who seem to have problems
not different from ours, nor do they behave well.
And where are they now? The lush world
surrounds us. Could it be that they, too,
felt like exiles in the midst
of almost unforgettable beauty,
and took up the long work of forgetting?

# Slow Work

You need something to tend that exacts a stately pace.
You could set type, dice vegetables for soup,
or knit a tiny sweater no faster than the baby

gestates for whom it's meant. Or translate Martial,
scrubbing the rust from your Latin. Then you could
spend a month in a writers' retreat, honing the barbed

tips of the stingers in Martial's undiligent
and antisocial bees, not Romans aswarm
but pains to be named later. You'd work on Martial

most of the day, time out for a thoughtful walk,
and sleep in a bed no wider than a stretcher
and dream of cognates and black smoke. The girl

on your left on the plane had explained
that her father was a shipping impresario
and had named a ship for her; she was on her way

back from whapping it on the butt with a magnum
of champagne. The woman on your right had asked
what you do when you finish a book. Write another?

Right she was. There's what we call the body of work
and it grows, by taken pains, suppler and more vivid.
The work of the body is to chafe and stiffen.

*E lucevan le stelle*


And the stars shone, and the earth unstoppered
its perfumes, the garden gate scrinched
open, footsteps lisped along the path
and they were hers, and she was mine.

And my hand shook the more slowly
I unwrapped and dawdlier I kissed her,
and her aromas rose, and the hour fled,
which is the way with hours.

And I've unveiled myself of any hope,
and death's steps rasp along the path,
and, like any star, I have nothing
to burn but the life I love.

# Portrait of the Artist as a Young Clarinetist

I was a dull musician as a boy —
I sucked a reed as if it were my thumb —
but did that make me mute? A strangled joy

burbled in me like an inept glory
that music might release if I weren't dumb.
I was a bad musician as a boy,

but a boy has grandeurs: *le jazz, c'est moi.*
No matter that this kingdom didn't come
because I couldn't toot my strangled joy.

Mine's not a sad but a well-known story:
the clarinet requires only two thumbs.
I was a drab musician as a boy.

"The clarinet, young man, is not a toy,"
my patient teacher barked, his calm undone
by some simple piece I'd mangled. Joy

grew from work, patience and melancholy,
I now think. Good thing I was so stubborn,
a poor musician even as a boy,
and destitute before my strangled joy.

# Debt

Money's job is to change hands fast, no flies
on it. As one in a bucket brigade —
and in each bucket a small rage of fire —
I pass it on. *Industry on Parade,*
they used to show us on gray grade-school days,
or *The Timken Ball Bearing Story:* garish
flames, fibrillating shadows, workers' faces
etched by sweat . . . Kettle drumbeats, flourishes
of brass, music for the war on matter . . .
The workers were in place and the products
on parade, just as we sat and the film
spooled by. They made cars and we made trouble,
faces, spitballs. If we ever grew up,
we'd pay for this, Mrs. Updike sputtered.

# Condoms Then

Trojan, Sheik — the names confirmed what we feared:
sex happened elsewhere to blatant raptors.
Condoms? Boyhood years, we called them rubbers.
Sometimes they broke, or slithered off, we heard,
if you "lost" your erection. (You don't
lose it, it melts. But then you may have seen
how pronouns slither, too: what do I mean
by "you"?) We carried them in our wallets
like rusting badges, or "shields," as the cops
say. "For protection from disease," the fine
print said. Walkers of dogs, mowers of grass,
rainy, blustering boys. "A piece of ass,"
we said, a slice of life. And who'd complain
about us? Wouldn't we soon grow up?

# Condoms Now

are like a good hex: wearing a surgeon's
mask into the subway, drinking only
bottled water (though it be packaged by
descendants of the corporate huns
who mucked our rivers and scumbled our air),
fending off the world that set our parents'
tables and compounded their retirement
funds. There's something poisonous out there
we can't let in — or if it's here, let loose.
The world is too much with us? Not if we
sift through it like anorectic ghosts.
Our smirched, AIDS-riven, only world accosts
us with its mottled, usual beauty
daily. Can't we both take care and rejoice?

# Phone Log

Sunday, 1:46 A.M., I'm up
tending the weedy garden of my desk
and the phone rings. No news at this hour's
good, so I try an insincere "Hello?"
There's a practiced pause and then a husked male
voice asks, the same flat stress on each word,
"How big is your cock?"

"You must have a wrong number," I quip,
and hang up, then sit half an hour thinking
what I might have said. "You mean right now?" Or,
"If you have to ask you can't afford it."
Or, ever the teacher, I might have plied
the Socratic method and asked him,
"How fleet is your pig?"

But next I think of dire phone calls I'd made
too late at night, drunk, curdled by regret
for my unloveliness, and how I'd known
as I picked up the phone, although I told
myself the opposite, that I had found
but a new way to reach out and touch my
old bone-loneliness.

# Driving Through the Poconos,
Route 80, 1:30 A.M., Snow

I pass the big rigs on the upgrades;
they measle me with roadslush on the downslopes.
Skeins of snowflakes waver in my headlights

like curtains in a draft. Of course I can't see
the swatches of black ice I speed across,
but I can feel a slur — a tiny, stifled

shimmy, faster than a thought — in my rear
tires. File cabinets and mattresses hurtle
downhill. Stroudsburg: 32 miles.

Enough butter to slather a county surges
past me. We bottom out. Carting a few
books and an extra pair of shoes, I pass

the butter. Semis doze in the rest areas,
the orange cab lights stippled by snow,
while we who are close enough to sleep

to keep on driving toward it, keep on
driving toward it, although we're neither
here (Stroudsburg: 11 miles) nor there.

# The Buddy Bolden Cylinder

It doesn't exist, I know, but I love
to think of it, wrapped in a shawl
or bridal veil, or, less dramatically,
in an old copy of the *Daily Picayune*,
and like an unstaled, unhatched egg
from which, at the right touch, like mine,
the legendary tone, sealed these long years
in the amber of neglect, would peal and re-
peal across the waters. What waters do
I have in mind? Nothing symbolic, mind you.
I meant the sinuous and filth-rich
Mississippi across which you could hear
him play from Gretna, his tone was so loud
and sweet, with a moan in it like you were
in church, and on those old, slow, low-down
blues Buddy could make the women jump
the way they liked. But it doesn't exist,
it never did, except as a relic
for a jazz hagiography, and all
we think we know about Bolden's music
is, really, a melancholy gossip
and none of it sown by Bolden, who
spent his last twenty-four years in Jackson
(Insane Asylum of Louisiana)
hearing the voices of people who spooked
him before he got there. There's more than one
kind of ghostly music in the air, all
of them like the wind: you can't see it
but you can see the leaves shiver in place
as if they'd like to turn their insides out.

# The Memo

*I want this up and running,* the office
bully wrote, *next Monday,* and *I insist
blah blah blah blah.* Each *blah* stands for three
or four moronic insistences, because
a poem honors the non-reading hours
in its readers' lives by brevity, just
as grace uses far less time than dinner.

And this poem, *presto,* replaces the memo.
Gentle reader, you didn't need that shit.
You work hard, right? You wanna be the screen
on which some bozo you don't know projects
his lurid drama, *Bozo: The Lean Years?*
Or do you want to control your leisure?
If so you'll want to take this simple test.

# Grandmother Talking

"Do the pelicans seem scarce to you?
The world is gorged with people and these poor
baggy, rumpled birds are fewer year
by year. They used to lurk—maybe to dry
their wings?—one to a dockpost all along
the bay. See how many posts are vacant?

I met a woman who's been twice married
to admirals but they both died. 'Well, you're
a killer,' I told her, 'aren't you?' And she
said, 'Yes, I am.' Well, what else could she say?
Cigarettes, I know now, stilled my husband's
heart and left me all this time. They're afraid

I'll fall on my back and squirm like a turtle
while no one comes, so I'm sentenced to this
walker. I hated to clump, but once I got
wheels for it I was off and dawdling,
going nowhere fast, since I'm going
somewhere so slow I often forget where

en route. I wish you'd stay longer, and your
pretty wife. You won't divorce her too, I hope?
Well, who'd have thought it, ninety-six? I packed
my heart like a sachet and married a man
from Cincinnati and look what it's all
come to. This, all of it, everything."

# Grandmother, Dead at 99 Years and 10 Months

Everyone cheered her on
like a race horse
to make a hundred,
but when I asked
how she felt, she said,
without pause, "Old."
Two by two the young
with their ambitious
jitters bought the houses
her friends died out of.
The village ate and ate
and cleared its plate.

"Dearie, what are you doing
here?" her husband, dead now
thirty years, asked me one
Thanksgiving in the garage,
each of us bearing a flute
of champagne, Veuve Clicquot.
I loved him and so told
the truth. "Hiding." "Me too,"
he said; "I want to bring
us all together here,
but the garage is part of here."
We clinked glasses and drank.

Like the widow Clicquot
she amazed the menfolk
and, more gallingly, outlived them,
including two of her three sons.
Tough as a turtle, everyone

said, but if she fell on her back . . .
She'd lost control of her
bowels, checkbook and legs,
and everyone cheered her on.
I raise a glass
to her truant kidney
and to oblivion.

# Names

Ten kinds of wolf are gone and twelve of rat
and not a single insect species.
Three sorts of skink are history and two
of minnow, two of pupfish, ten of owl.
Seventeen kinds of rail are out of here
and five of finch. It comforts us to think
the dinosaurs bought their farms all at once,
but they died at a rate of one species
per thousand years. Life in a faster lane
erased the speckled dace, the thicktail chub,
two kinds of thrush and six of wren, the heath
hen and Ash Meadows killfish. There are four
kinds of sucker not born any minute
anymore. The Christmas Island musk shrew
is defunct. Some places molt and peel so fast
it's a wonder they have any name:
the Chatham Island bellbird flew the coop
as did the Chatham Island fernbird, the
Lord Howe Island fantail and the Lord Howe
Island blackbird. The Utah Lake sculpin,
Arizona jaguar and Puerto
Rican caviomorph, the Vegas Valley
leopard frog and New Caledonian lorikeet?
They've hit the road for which there is no name
a mouth surrounds so well as it did theirs.
The sea mink's crossed the bar and the great auk's
ground time here was brief. Four forms the macaw
took are canceled checks. Sad Adam fills his lungs
with haunted air, and so does angry Eve:
they meant no name they made up for farewell.
They were just a couple starting out,

a place they could afford, a few laughs,
no champagne but a bottle of rosé.
In fact Adam and Eve are not their names.

# I Let a Song Go out of My Heart

I bruised my beloved's heart
by inattention and saw the smolder
in her eyes, too late, of course, for
hadn't I taught myself not to watch
myself not pay attention to her?

And for what? The sump of silence,
the tatty ruths of loneliness.
When love drew near I threw salt
over my shoulder. *Accidente.*
For dross, for cigarette ash, for the scent

of my own farts. For dust to which we must
all return, but to which we need not speed.
Once the siege is done, the fort becomes a prison.
So I've made this dirge by which I can
begin to teach myself to sing again.

# After All
## (1998)

# Mingus in Shadow

What you see in his face in the last
photograph, when ALS had whittled
his body to fit a wheelchair, is how much
stark work it took to fend death off, and fail.
The famous rage got eaten cell by cell.

His eyes are drawn to slits against the glare
of the blanched landscape. The day he died,
the story goes, a swash of dead whales
washed up on the Baja beach. Great nature grieved
for him, the story means, but it was great

nature that skewed his cells and siphoned
his force and melted his fat like tallow
and beached him in a wheelchair under
a sombrero. It was human nature,
tiny nature, to take the photograph,

to fuss with the aperture and speed, to let
in the right blare of light just long enough
to etch pale Mingus to the negative.
In the small, memorial world of that
negative, he's all the light there is.

# Rescue

To absolve me of my loneliness, and rather
than board her for the stint, I brought
my cat with me for two weeks in Vermont. Across
bare, borrowed floors she harried ping-
pong balls, her claws like castanets, her blunt face rapt—
she kept a ball ahead of her
and between her paws as she chased it full tilt.

Then she'd amble over to where I sat reading
and stretch her utmost length against
my flank and let her heartbeat diminish until
she dozed. So long as she knew where
in that strange space I was, and up to what, she could
make it hers. When I stepped into
eclipse behind an opaque shower curtain, not

at all like the translucent booth she peers into
to watch the blur lather and rinse
himself at home, and when I turned a different
torrent loose, she must have leapt
to the lid of the toilet tank, and measured what next,
rocking back on her haunches,
then forward, and back again, and then the flying

hoyden launched herself at the rod the shower curtain's
strung along, landing, *clank,* only two
or three inches off, and hung there held up by her
forearms, if a cat has forearms,
like the least fit student in gym class quitting on
a chin-up. Her rear paws churned egg-
beater style. And then what? If I pulled her toward

me with wet, soapy hands, she'd thrash and slash herself
free, but free in a tub. Hung up
as she was, she had nothing to push off from, so
she'd have to let herself drop, *clunk,*
and turn to the torn curtain her I-meant-to-do-
that face, while, slick and pink, I called
out from the other side, "Sweet cat, are you OK?"

# Truffle Pigs

None of these men, who all run truffle pigs,
compares a truffle to itself. "Fossil
testicles," says one. And another: "No.
Inky, tiny brains, smart only about
money." They like to say, "You get yourself

a pig like this, you've got a live pension."
The dowsing sows sweep their flat snouts across
the scat and leaf rot, scurf and duff, the slow
fires of decay. They know what to ignore;
these pigs are innocent of metaphor.

Tumor, fetus, truffle — all God's creatures
jubilate to grow. Even the diffident truffle
gives off a faint sweat from the joyful work
of burgeoning, and by that spoor the pigs
have learned to know them and to root them out.

# Manners

"Sweetypants," Martha Mitchell (wife of John
Mitchell, soon to be Nixon's attorney general)
cried, "fetch me a glass of bubbin,
won't you?" Out of office, Nixon
had been warehoused in Leonard Garment's
New York law firm and had begun to clamber

his way back toward Washington.
The scent of his enemies' blood rose
hotly from the drinks that night.
Why was I there? A college class-
mate's mother had suggested he invite a few
friends; she called us "starving scholars."

It's hard to do good and not advertise
yourself, and not to need the needy
even if they don't need you. I'd grown used
to being accused of being somewhere else.
I plied my nose, that shrewd scout, into book
after book at home, and clattered downstairs

for dinner not late but tardy. I dwelt
as much as I could at that remove
from the needs of others we call "the self,"
that desert isle, that Alcatraz from which
none has escaped. I made a happy lifer.
There is no frigate like a book.

"Outside of a dog, a book is a man's
best friend," said Groucho Marx. "Inside of a dog,
it's too dark to read." So what if my friend's

mother was a fool. So what if Martha
Mitchell would later rat on her rat
of a husband when Nixon's paranoid

domain collapsed under its own venal
weight and it took Nixon all his gloomy
charisma to load his riven heart
onto a helicopter and yaw upward
from the White House lawn. He might have turned
to Pat and asked, like a child on a first

flight, "Are we getting smaller yet?"
I was too young to know how much I was,
simply by being born, a hostage
to history. My hostess's chill,
insulting grace I fended off with the same
bland good manners I used to stay upstairs

in my head until time had come for food.
A well-fed scholar, I sought out and brought
back a tall bubbin for the nice lady.
Yes, there's a cure for youth, but it's fatal.
And a cure for grace: you say what you mean,
but of course you have to know what that is.

# Promiscuous

"Mixes easily," dictionaries
used to say, a straight shot from the Latin.
Chemists applied the term to matter's
amiability.

But the *Random House Dictionary*
(1980) gives as its prime meaning:
"characterized
by frequent and indiscriminate

changes of one's sexual partners." Sounds
like a long way
to say "slut," that glob of blame we once threw
equally at men and women, all who slurred,

slavered, slobbered,
slumped, slept or lapsed, slunk or relapsed, slackened
(loose lips sink ships) or slubbed, or slovened. But soon
a slut was female. A much-bedded male

got called a ladies' man; he never slept
with sluts. How sluts
got to be sluts is thus a mystery,
except the language knows what we may

have forgot. "Depression" began its career
in English in 1656, says
the *OED*,
and meant (science jargon) the opposite

of elevation—a hole or a rut,
perhaps, or, later, "the angular

distance of a celestial object
below the horizon,"

as *Webster's Third* (1963)
has it. There's ample record of our self-
deceit: language,
that furious river, carries on its foamed

and sinewed back all we thought we'd shucked off.
Of course it's all
pell-mell, head over heels, snickers and grief,
love notes and libel, fire and ice. In short:

promiscuous.

# Sooey Generous

Saint Anthony, patron of sausage makers,
guide my pen and unkink my tongue. Of swine
I sing, and of those who tend and slaughter them,
of slops and wallows and fodder, of piglets
doddering on their stilty legs, and sows
splayed to offer burgeoned teats to sucklers,
and the four to five tons of manure
a pig (that ambling buffet) reinvests
in the soil each year; of truffle dowsers
and crunchers of chestnuts and acorns I sing.

In medieval Naples, each household
kept a pig on a twenty-four-foot tether,
rope enough that the hooved Hoover could
scour the domain, whereas in Rome
pigs foraged the streets haunted today by
rat-thin cats, tendons with fur. In Paris
in those years the *langueyers,* the "tonguers,"
or meat inspectors, lifted a pig's tongue
to look for white ulcers, since the comely
pig in spoiled condition could poison

a family. Indeed the Buddha died
from eating spoiled pork, vegetarians
I know like to insist, raising the stakes
from wrong to fatal, gleefully. Perhaps
you've read the bumper sticker too: *A Heart
Attack Is God's Revenge for Eating His
Little Friends.* Two major religions
prohibit eating pork. Both creeds were forged
in deserts, and the site-specific pig,
who detests dry mud, has never mixed well

with nomads or vice versa. Since a pig
eats everything, just as the cuisines that
sanctify the pig discard no fragment
of it, it makes sense to eat it whole hog
or shun it altogether, since to eat
or not to eat is sacral, if there's a choice
in the matter. To fast is not to starve.
The thirteen ravenous, sea-queasy pigs
Hernando de Soto loosed near Tampa
in 1542 ate whatever

they liked. How glad they must have been to hoove
some soil after skidding in the slick hold
week after dark week: a pig without sun
on its sullied back grows skittish and glum.
Pigs and pioneers would build America.
Cincinnati was called Porkopolis
in the 1830s; the hogs arrived,
as the hunger for them had, by river,
from which a short forced march led to slaughter.
A new country travels on its belly,

and manufacture starts in the barnyard:
hide for leather and stomach for pepsin.
In France, a farm family calls its pig
"Monsieur." According to a CIA
tally early in 1978,
the Chinese kept 280 million
of the world's 400 million pigs;
perhaps all of them were called "The Chairman."
Emmaeus, swineherd to Odysseus,
guarded 600 sows and their litters

(the males slept outside), and no doubt each sow
and piglet had its own name in that rich
matriarchal mire. And I like to think
that in that mild hospice future pork roasts

fattened toward oblivion with all
the love and dignity that husbandry
has given up to be an industry,
and that the meat of Emmaeus's coddled
porkers tasted a little sweeter for
the graces of affection and a name.

# Oxymorons

Summer school, and *jumbo shrimp*, of course.
*Friendly fire, famous poet, common sense*,
and, until very recently, *safe sex.*
*Blind date, sure thing, amicable divorce.*

Also there's *loyal opposition*,
*social security, deliberate speed.*
How about *dysfunctional family?*
Eyes blackened, hearts crushed, the damn thing functions.

Some things we say should coat our tongues with ash.
*Drug-Free School Zone?* No way: it's our money
our children toke, snort and shoot up while we
vote against higher property taxes.

Want a one-word oxymoron? *Prepay.*
Money's — forgive me — rich in such mischief:
*trust officer, debt service, common thief* —
these phrases all want to have it both ways

and sag at the middle like decrepit beds.
*Religious freedom* — doesn't that sound good?
And some *assisted living* when we're old
and in our cryptic dreams the many dead

swirl like a fitful snow. We'll wake and not
think of our *living wills* or property.
We'll want some breakfast. Our memories
will be our *real estate,* all that we've got.

# Dire Cure

"First, do no harm," the Hippocratic
Oath begins, but before she might enjoy
such balm, the docs had to harm her tumor.
It was large, rare and so anomalous
in its behavior that at first they mis-
diagnosed it. "Your wife will die of it
within a year." But in ten days or so
I sat beside her bed with hot and sour
soup and heard an intern congratulate
her on her new diagnosis: a children's

cancer (doesn't that possessive break
your heart?) had possessed her. I couldn't stop
personifying it. Devious, dour,
it had a clouded heart, like Iago's.
It loved disguise. It was a garrison
in a captured city, a bad horror film
(*The Blob*), a stowaway, an inside job.
If I could make it be like something else,
I wouldn't have to think of it as what,
in fact, it was: part of my lovely wife.

Next, then, chemotherapy. Her hair fell
out in tufts, her color dulled, she sat laced
to bags of poison she endured somewhat
better than her cancer cells could, though not
by much. And indeed, the cancer cells waned
more slowly than the chemical "cocktails"
(one the bright color of Campari), as the chemo
nurses called them, dripped into her. There were
three hundred days of this: a week inside
the hospital and two weeks out, the fierce

elixirs percolating all the while.
She did five weeks of radiation, too,
Monday to Friday like a stupid job.
She wouldn't eat the food the hospital
wheeled in. "Puréed fish" and "minced fish" were worth,
I thought, a sharp surge of food snobbery,
but she'd grown averse to it all — the nurses'
crepe soles' muffled squeaks along the hall,
the filtered air, the smothered urge to read,
the fear, the perky visitors, flowers

she'd not been sent when she was well, the room-
mate (what do "semi-private" and "extra
virgin" have in common?) who died, the nights
she wept and sweated faster than the tubes
could moisten her with pretty poison.
One chemotherapy veteran, six
years in remission, chanced on her former
chemo nurse at a bus stop and threw up.
My wife's tumor has not come back.
I like to think of it in Tumor Hell,

strapped to a dray, flat as a deflated
football, bleak and nubbled like a poorly
ironed truffle. There's one tense in Tumor Hell,
forever, or what we call the present.
For that long the flaccid tumor marinates
in lurid toxins. Tumor Hell Clinic
is, it turns out, a teaching hospital.
Every century or so, the way
we'd measure it, a chief doc brings a pack
of students round. They run some simple tests:

surge current through the tumor, batter it
with mallets, push a woodplane across its
pebbled hide and watch a scurf of tumor-
pelt kink loose from it, impale it, strafe it

with lye and napalm. There might be nothing
left in there but a still space surrounded
by a carapace. "This one is nearly
dead," the lead doc says. "What's the cure for that?"
The students know: "Kill it slower, of course."
They sprinkle it with rock salt and move on.

Here on the aging earth the tumor's gone:
my wife is hale, though wary, and why not?
Once you've had cancer, you don't get headaches
anymore, you get brain tumors, at least
until the aspirin kicks in. Her hair's back,
her weight, her appetite. "And what about you?"
friends ask me. First the fear felt like sudden
weightlessness: I couldn't steer and couldn't stay.
I couldn't concentrate: surely my spit would
dry before I could slather a stamp.

I made a list of things to do next day
before I went to bed, slept like a cork,
woke to no more memory of last night's
list than smoke has of fire, made a new list,
began to do the things on it, wept, paced,
berated myself, drove to the hospital
and brought my wife food from the take-out joints
that ring a hospital as surely as
brothels surround a gold strike. I drove home
rancid with anger at her luck and mine —

anger that filled me the same way nature
hates a vacuum. "This must be hell for you,"
some said. Hell's not other people: Sartre
was wrong about that, too. *L'enfer, c'est moi?*
I've not got the ego for it. There'd be
no hell if Dante hadn't built a model
of his rage so well, and he contrived to
get exiled from it, for it was Florence.

Why would I live in hell? I love New York.
Some even said the tumor and fierce cure

were harder on the caregiver — yes, they
said "caregiver" — than on the "sick person."
They were wrong who said those things. Of course
I hated it, but some of "it" was me —
the self-pity I allowed myself,
the brave poses I struck. The rest was dire
threat my wife met with moral stubbornness,
terror, rude jokes, nausea, you name it.
No, let her think of its name and never
say it, as if it were the name of God.

# Umbrian Nightfall

The stench-rich stones dogs parse all day will reek
all night of data, but one
by one the dogs get summoned home. Streetlights
sizzle on and bats unfurl.
The Tiber valley, trough of a thousand
shades of green, has brimmed with dusk.
It's late. High time. High ground. Even the hill-
top towns stand tiptoe. The lake
of the black night laps everywhere. Two dogs
(three?), like raddled islands, bark.

# The Cloister

The last light of a July evening drained
into the streets below. My love and I had hard
things to say and hear, and we sat over
wine, faltering, picking our words carefully.

The afternoon before I had lain across
my bed and my cat leapt up to lie
alongside me, purring and slowly
growing dozy. By this ritual I could

clear some clutter from my baroque brain.
And into that brief vacancy the image
of a horse cantered, coming straight to me,
and I knew it brought hard talk and hurt

and fear. How did we do? A medium job,
which is well above average. But because
she had opened her heart to me as far
as she did, I saw her fierce privacy,

like a gnarled, luxuriant tree all hung
with disappointments, and I knew
that to love her I must love the tree
and the nothing it cares for me.

# A Poetry Reading at West Point

I read to the entire plebe class,
in two batches. Twice the hall filled
with bodies dressed alike, each toting
a copy of my book. What would my
shrink say, if I had one, about
such a dream, if it were a dream?

Question-and-answer time.
"Sir," a cadet yelled from the balcony,
and gave his name and rank, and then,
closing his parentheses, yelled
"Sir" again. "Why do your poems give
me a headache when I try

to understand them?" he asked. "Do
you want that?" I have a gift for
gentle jokes to defuse tension,
but this was not the time to use it.
"I try to write as well as I can
what it feels like to be human,"

I started, picking my way care-
fully, for he and I were, after
all, pained by the same dumb longings.
"I try to say what I don't know
how to say, but of course I can't
get much of it down at all."

By now I was sweating bullets.
"I don't want my poems to be hard,
unless the truth is, if there is

a truth." Silence hung in the hall
like a heavy fabric. Now my
head ached. "Sir," he yelled. "Thank you. Sir."

# People Like Us

When the ox was the gray enemy
of the forest and engine of the plow,
the poor drifted across the fields,
through the sweet grasses and the vile,
and tendered bare bowls at our doors.
We hoarded and they begged. We piled
ricks high with hay and they slept there
like barn cats or cuckoos.

When we sluiced the maculate streets
with fermenting slops, and strode to our jobs
furred by coal dust, didn't the poor
punctuate our routines with cries
for alms? Our sclerotic rivers
turned the color of old leather
and the poor fished them anyway
and slept under their bridges.

Now they come surging up the stairs
and up the fire escapes. Open our door
to them and then they're us,
and if we don't we're trapped inside
with only us for company
while in the hall they pray and sing
their lilting anthems of reproach
while we bite our poor tongues.

# Frazzle

"All for one and one for all" was our motto after all
our tribulations. And then we'd each go home, after all.

By the people. For the people. Of the people. Grammar—
but politics is an incomplete sentence, after all.

"Better to have loved and lost . . . ," the poet wrote.
Than to have won? Poetry dotes on loss, after all.

They don't take the flag down at dusk, the patriot grumbled.
A country's too big to love, but not a rule, after all.

How would you translate "self-service" or "lube job"
if you had a dirty mind and scant English, after all?

Veil (beekeeper's? bridal?), Vale (tears), Vail (Colorado).
Phonics? No avail. Better learn to spell, after all.

The love of repetition is the root of all form?
Well, liturgy and nonsense are cousins, after all.

"I cannot tell a lie," he said, which was a lie,
but not the kind for which the bill comes after all.

# The Bar at the Andover Inn

*May 28, 1995*

The bride, groom (my son), and their friends gathered
somewhere else to siphon the wedding's last
drops from their tired elders. Over a glass
of chardonnay I ignored my tattered,
companionable glooms (this took some will:
I've ended three marriages by divorce
as a man shoots his broken-legged horse)
and wished my two sons and their families
something I couldn't have, or keep, myself.
The rueful pluck we take with us to bars
or church, the morbid fellowship of woe —
I've had my fill of it. I wouldn't mope
through my son's happiness or further fear
my own. Well, what instead? Well, something else.

# Big Tongue

The spit-sheathed shut-in, sometimes
civil, lolls on its leash in its cave
between meals, blunt little *feinschmecker.*
He seems both sullen and proud, not
an unusual combination. Well, that little
blind boy knows his way around the mouth.
An aspirate here, a glottal stop there —
he's a blur. He works to make sensible
noise at least as hard as an organist,
and so giddily pleased by his own

skill that for the sheer bravura
of it he flicks a shard of chicken
salad free from a molar *en route*
to the startling but exact finish
of a serpentine and pleasing sentence.
God knows the brain deserves most
of the credit for the sentence, but then
wasn't it God who insisted from the first
that whatever "it" means, it isn't fair?
Theology can be stored in a couplet:

The reason God won't answer you
is God has better things to do.

I mention only briefly, *mia diletta,*
lest I embarrass you by lingering,
how avidly this tongue nuzzled your nub,
how slowly (glib is his day job) he urged
your pleased clamor. Think then how he might feel —
the spokesman, the truffle pig, Mr. Muscle —

to sense along the length of his savor
a hard node, like a knot in a tree, and thus
to know another attack's begun. First one
side of the bilateral tongue will stiffen

and swell to two or three times normal size
(it's like having a small shoe in your mouth),
and then, as it subsides, after three or four
hours, the other side grows grandiose.
(Your salivary glands are like grapes
on steroids. Your speech is feral — only vowels,
and those from no language you recognize.)
Pride goeth before a bloat. Start to puff yourself up
and next thing you know you'll be on TV,
in the Macy's parade. *Vae, puto deus fio*

("Damn, I think I'm becoming a god," said
the emperor Vespasian on his deathbed).

But let's bring this descant back down to earth:
names ground us, and this humiliation's called
angioedema, short (?!) for angioneurotic
edema, often "an expression of allergy,"
as *Webster's Third* has it. What's the humbled
tongue, sore from strenuous burgeon and wane,
allergic to? Whatever it is, it may well be
systemic, and the "attack" a kind of defense,
a purge, a violent recapture of balance,
like a migraine or an epileptic seizure.

"Who needs this?" I might cry out. The answer
might be: I do. So why am I exchanging vows
with my allergies? Although I hate it when my
competence is sick, I hereby refuse
to make mine allegorical, though not before,
you'll note, I've had my fun with that possibility —
for where's "the bribe of pleasure" (as Dr. Freud,

that gloomy *mensch,* called it) in being sick
if I can't loll in limelight for a while?
Where next? My dressing room, to wipe off the drama

and stare at the mirror,
met by ordinary fear.

# Bucket's Got a Hole in It

Keep it under your hat, the saying went
when we wore hats. And secrets dissipate
(in this poem the verb means "to leave the pate")
like body heat. And some secrets can't quit
memory fast enough for human good;
viz., what my friend's wife's kisses tasted like

and why I didn't sleep with her for all
her vernal allure. Did we need to read
in transcript each taped word of Nixon's
contempt for us, like preserved globs of spit?
Don't double-click on the Save icon
(a piggy bank? a jumbled attic?)

until you've thought how much a fossil fuel
has to forget fossil to become fuel,
or how much childhood we plow under.
"Tears, idle tears," the poet wrote, but they've
got their work cut out for them, the way
a river might imagine a canyon.

# Misgivings

"Perhaps you'll tire of me," muses
my love, although she's like a great city
to me, or a park that finds new
ways to wear each flounce of light
and investiture of weather.
Soil doesn't tire of rain, I think,

but I know what she fears: plans warp,
planes explode, topsoil gets peeled away
by floods. And worse than what we can't
control is what we could; those drab,
scuttled marriages we shed so
gratefully may augur we're on our own

for good reasons. "Hi, honey," chirps Dread
when I come through the door, "you're home."
Experience is a great teacher
of the value of experience,
its claustrophobic prudence,
its gloomy name-the-disasters-

in-advance charisma. Listen,
my wary one, it's far too late
to unlove each other. Instead let's cook
something elaborate and not
invite anyone to share it but eat it
all up very very slowly.

# Care

The lump of coal my parents teased
I'd find in my Christmas stocking
turned out each year to be an orange,
for I was their sunshine.

Now I have one C. gave me,
a dense node of sleeping fire.
I keep it where I read and write.
"You're on chummy terms with dread,"

it reminds me. "You kiss ambivalence
on both cheeks. But if you close your
heart to me ever, I'll wreathe you in flames
and convert you to energy."

I don't know what C. meant me to mind
by her gift, but the sun returns
unbidden. Books get read and written.
My mother comes to visit. My father's

dead. Love needs to be set alight
again and again, and in thanks
for tending it, will do its very
best not to consume us.

# INDEX OF TITLES